The depth of Soul Survivor's experience in youth ministry is finally available for youth groups everywhere! Soul Survivor Encounter utilizes the gospel to energize your students, impassion your leaders and immerse your community in the values of service, relationship, worship, justice and evangelism. Don't miss out on this series of truly fantastic resources!

Josh McDowell
Speaker
Author, *Evidence That Demands a Verdict*

Soul Survivor is undoubtedly in the center of this generation's fresh wind of the Spirit. The message is clear and spiritually motivating. This material is wonderful.

Jim Burns
Founder and President, YouthBuilders

When a devotional starts with quotes from Bono, Avril Lavigne or Mel Gibson, something's up. In the case of Soul Survivor Encounter, that something is starting with youths' real lives, not with a religious subculture. A refreshing mix of classical theology with feet firmly planted in the neighborhood.

Sally Morgenthaler
Speaker
Founder, Sacramentis.com
and Digital Glass Videos

There is no greater challenge facing us today than to engage emerging generations with the truths of the Scriptures, and Soul Survivor Encounter hits the bull's-eye in how to go about doing that.

Dan Kimball
Author, *The Emerging Church: Vintage Christianity
for New Generations*
Pastor, Vintage Faith Church,
Santa Cruz, California

Soul Survivor is a win-win resource. Youth leaders win with user-friendly resources that bring depth to their ministries. Students win with engaging discussion and reflection tools that help connect the dots between their faith and their life.

Kara Powell
Executive Director, Fuller Seminary Center
for Ministry to Youth and Their Families

From the start, Soul Survivor Encounter grabs you and doesn't let go. This new series of materials for students is grounded in the Bible, in touch with the world, full of activities and ideas; a truly interactive thrill for students and their youth leaders!

Darlene Zschech
Worship Leader

Soul Survivor Encounter hits kids where they are on several levels. It is culturally current, interactive, community building and solidly biblical. It brings God's Word right into the teenage world with personal stories, practical application and action steps. It moves from information to transformation and is hip without being flip. With journaling, projects and daily devotions, the Christian life becomes whole, rather than an isolated Sunday experience. Most of all Jesus, the eternal Son of God, is presented as the compelling Lord to be worshiped and a friend to share life with 24/7.

Don Williams, Ph.D.
Speaker
Author, *Twelve Steps with Jesus*

soul survivor

encounter

Guide to Youth Ministry

MIKE PILAVACHI

GENERAL EDITOR

Gospel Light

Gospel Light

Gospel Light is a Christian publisher dedicated to serving the local church. We believe God's vision for Gospel Light is to provide church leaders with biblical, user-friendly materials that will help them evangelize, disciple and minister to children, youth and families.

It is our prayer that this Gospel Light resource will help you discover biblical truth for your own life and help you minister to youth. May God richly bless you.

For a free catalog of resources from Gospel Light, please contact your Christian supplier or contact us at 1-800-4-GOSPEL *or* www.gospellight.com.

PUBLISHING STAFF

William T. Greig, Chairman

Dr. Elmer L. Towns, Senior Consulting Publisher

Natalie Clark, Product Line Manager

Pam Weston, Managing Editor

Alex Field, Associate Editor

Jessie Minassian, Editorial Assistant

Bayard Taylor, M.Div., Senior Editor, Biblical and Theological Issues

Mike Pilavachi, General Editor

Steve Nicholson, Gareth Dickinson, Aaron Adams, Charlotte Beavis, Pete Hughes, Jack Cleverly, Beverly Friend, Rachel Shorey, Emily Layzell, Martin Layzell, David Trevor, Paul Daniels, David Westlake, Chris Bullivant, Si Jones, Mark Meardon, Mike Resch, Sarah Norris, Emma Mitchell, Contributors

Samantha Hsu, Art Director

Zelle Olson, Designer

ISBN 0-8307-3530-5
© 2004 Gospel Light,
All rights reserved.
Printed in the U.S.A.

Contents

Introduction

The aim of *Soul Survivor Guide to Youth Ministry* is to share the things we've learned over the years at Soul Survivor, both through trial and error, and through contact with various youth organizations and leaders around the world. We hope that you will find this book a useful, practical tool to help you develop leaders and volunteers for ministry.

People often ask us to share our ministry secrets for raising up young leaders. We'll be the first to say that there isn't any one way! But we do believe that good leadership is essential to the growth of the Church and its subsequent rise or fall. We also believe that now is the time to encourage, develop and release new leaders in churches around the world. This book's purpose isn't to help you create your own Soul Survivor; rather, its purpose is to outline the principles of successful youth ministry that we've stumbled across and to encourage you with stories that will help your own unique ministry excel.

This book is divided into two sections. The first section recounts a detailed history of Soul Survivor Watford, describes the evolution of Soul Survivor's most ambitious festival to date, The Message 2000, and explores the idea of youth church.

The second section focuses specifically on leadership and the training and releasing of young leaders within your church, ministry or youth group. We transcribed this invaluable section from talks given by Steve Nicholson, senior pastor of Evanston Vineyard Church in Illinois. Steve is a very good friend of Soul Survivor, and our ministry as a whole has learned a great deal from his expertise.

Whether you use the materials in this book for training young leaders, to prepare a project or simply for your own information, our prayer is that God would be glorified through your use of this book in your local context. Blessings to you as you seek God's calling in your life.

soul survivor

Part One

Chapter One

THE HISTORY OF SOUL SURVIVOR

Soul Survivor Watford is a missionary congregation that reaches out to young people and a church plant of Saint Andrew's Church in Chorleywood, England.

OUR BEGINNINGS

In the beginning, Mike Pilavachi was based at Saint Andrew's Church where he was on staff for seven years, first as the youth leader and then in a variety of other roles. After getting involved in the youth program at New Wine, a family conference birthed out of Saint Andrew's, he saw the need for young people to have their own event. Young people needed an event where they could worship, hear teaching, do ministry with other Christians their age and be encouraged that they were not alone as young Christians.

The first youth event took place in rural Shepton Mallet in the summer of 1993 and Mike and his team decided to call it Soul Survivor. Since then it has grown into an event that nearly 20,000 young people attend

each summer, an event where kids gather for worship, teaching, ministry and a whole lineup of activities and events.

From the start, Mike also felt a call to become more personally involved with youth work as he saw how many young people were hurting and broken in the Church! With as many as 300 young people a week leaving churches throughout Europe, he knew that action was needed and soon.

Eleven

Mike shared his desire with some of the young people around him and found that there was a group of people who shared his vision. So in September 1993, 11 people met in a living room to discuss the possibilities for reaching young people. About half of them were from Saint Andrew's Church in Chorleywood and the other half from Saint Andrew's Church in Watford, a church plant of Chorleywood. We spent the first meeting in worship and prayer for young people. At this time, one of the people in the group had a vision that time was running out.

Each of the 11 had a heart and vision to tackle this vision on a local level, but no one had any idea where to start or what to do.

Watford

Watford was chosen as the home for Soul Survivor for the following three reasons:

- According to local census information, there were 24,000 people between the ages of 14 and 25 in the Watford area, of which an estimated 700 had contact with the Church.
- Watford was close to the team's base and had the support of both Saint Andrew's Chorleywood and Saint Andrew's Watford.
- The team had some experience working in Watford and it was known to be a center for young people.

OUR VISION

The team finally established the following vision statement:

Soul Survivor Watford is a group of Christians aiming to communicate the good news of Jesus Christ to the young people in Watford.

The primary aim of Soul Survivor Watford is to extend God's kingdom, particularly among young people, and to equip others to do the same. In addition, as part of that overall vision, the team believes that God has called them to do the following:

- Reach unchurched young people and those who might have left the Church and establish a worshiping, evangelizing, discipling and caring community among them.
- Encourage similar works in other places either by working out of Soul

Survivor Watford or by aiding and encouraging other like-minded groups.

OUR VALUES

Our values are the genetic code of our church, underpinning all that we seek to do. Specifically, Soul Survivor's values are intimate worship, quality relationships and relevant evangelism.

Intimate Worship

We believe that Christianity is all about relationship with God. It's not about rules and regulations—it's about knowing Him. This is the most important value for us and it's expressed in the following ways:

- We worship God with the whole of our lives, in thankfulness to Him.
- We worship God musically and by expressing His love to others.

Quality Relationships

The way we live our lives and how we treat others is a big part of our worship to God. Quality relationships are important and we do all we can to enhance our relationships and build people up. Our meetings seek to help people form and develop friendships and provide an environment of mutual support, care and community. We prize honesty and vulnerability and believe that all people need God's help.

Relevant Evangelism

We believe that relevant evangelism is not about how we use the latest technological fashions but about how to reach people by building relationships.

Our philosophy of evangelism seeks to make young people feel that they *belong* first and come to *believe* later, after which we hope their *behavior* will change. Many churches these days reverse this process by demanding that young people change their behavior before they believe. Then, only when they behave in the correct way and believe in Jesus, are they finally made to feel as if they belong.

Figure 1

BELONG ➡ BELIEVE ➡ BEHAVE

We strongly believe that we need to earn the right to speak to young people by showing them love and commitment, whether or not they become Christians. Once they feel that they belong, they're more likely to ask us questions about their beliefs, which is much easier than trying to provide answers to questions they're not asking.

Just because we don't concentrate on behavior first doesn't mean that we don't have any rules. It simply means that there are fewer rules and those rules cover whatever is necessary for being together.

OUR GROWTH

In January 1994, after we finalized the vision and a group of 20 had started to meet weekly to pray, we started Dreggs. Dreggs is a club with a café atmosphere where young people can gather for conversation and music. We took the idea from the atmosphere created at the youth portion of the New Wine conference.

We advertised Dreggs in the local schools, concentrating on kids aged 14 and older, inviting the kids to attend. The core team ran activities in the club-café, which included live bands, videos and computer games. The aim of these evenings was simply to create a safe, loving and friendly atmosphere for young people. In order to ensure that the young people went away feeling loved, the core team made every effort to build relationships.

On the first evening, only two people attended in addition to the core group. The following week word got out and more came along, and it grew from there.

As Dreggs grew, some local schools invited Mike Pilavachi to speak at their assemblies. Instead of preaching a gospel message, Mike gave short talks on values or the importance of self-worth. The schools also gave us the opportunity to bring in a band during lunchtime. We established relationships with six schools, and large numbers of the students began to attend Dreggs.

Another event at Dreggs was the monthly outing. Once a month, young people went on a field trip somewhere outside the Watford area with the Dreggs crew. The monthly outings provided further opportunities to chat with non-Christians and encouraged teamwork as we divided students into teams with Soul Survivor team members.

As time went on, Dreggs became well known, and nearly 100 people who were not part of Soul Survivor Watford attended regularly. Several of them even made commitments without ever having gone to church. The key seemed to be relationship building and simply feeling loved. The following is what a girl named Alice said about how Dreggs brought her to Jesus:

> For me, the thing that stood out at Dreggs was the sense that I wasn't just part of a project. When I spoke to the people and told them stuff about me, not only did they not tell others all my secrets, they would actually listen to what I had to say and then ask how things were going—sometimes weeks after the initial conversation. They actually seemed to want to know what was going on with me. It was something I'd not experienced before.

Dreggs continued to grow, changing venues four times—sometimes due to growth and other times due to the venue being unsuitable. Throughout this time we learned that we had to be flexible in our style and approach (i.e., lighting, décor and music volume) and Dreggs naturally evolved in those areas.

Monthly Celebrations

Not long after Dreggs began, Soul Survivor started holding monthly celebrations. Part of the purpose was to create an opportunity for Soul Survivor Watford members to minister to young people in a wider area than Watford. We designed these celebrations to be worship meetings that encouraged guests to take what they learned back to their own communities.

Another purpose for the monthly celebrations was to present the gospel to the young people we met in the schools and at Dreggs through worship and teaching in an un-threatening environment. This approach worked well.

The format of the youth-friendly celebrations was very simple. There was an extended time of worship in song (about 40 minutes), an evangelistic talk (about 15 minutes) and a ministry time at which we invited the Holy Spirit to come and move. The emphasis throughout the celebration was on being real.

We held these celebrations in a school hall. Due to the number of people attending and the low lighting, it was possible for people to check out the service while remaining relatively anonymous. The band that played at Dreggs led worship at the monthly celebrations, giving non-Christians who had been to Dreggs something tangible to relate to.

Although the talks were as accessible as possible, it actually proved to be the worship and ministry time that people responded to the most.

Soultime

Not long after the monthly celebrations began, the first Body Builders (now known as Soultime), a six-month discipleship course, began. Body Builders equipped young Christians by providing them with practical teaching that would allow them to live lives worthy of the gospel.

The first Body Builders group had 12 students dedicated to the vision of Soul Survivor Watford. As the core community of Soul Survivor Watford grew, the leaders formed more relationships on the weekends at Dreggs and continued those relationships throughout the week. The Body Builders students spent time during the week meeting with the young people they met at Dreggs or at the schools, growing friendships and helping disciple their new friends who were embarking on their own personal relationship with God.

The Soultime course has since been developed even further with a specific bias toward equipping young people for leadership and church planting.

Cell Groups

As attendance at Dreggs and at the celebrations grew, Soul Survivor Watford expanded. During this time, the team met every week in a team member's house for worship and prayer. By January 1995, however, Soul Survivor Watford numbered over 100 people, made up of converts from outreach events and other Christians who had moved into the area to join us.

To successfully maintain the sense of intimate community that characterized the church at the outset, we established five cell groups that met every other week in various homes for worship, teaching and ministry.

With the large number of people from outside the church attending the monthly celebrations, it became important to provide an opportunity for the cell groups to come together to deepen relationships and community within the church. These cluster meetings provided the opportunity for the five cell groups to come together every other week for collective worship, teaching and ministry. Church members attending a cluster meeting could join in conversation with others they hadn't met before, knowing that these people weren't merely visitors they'd never see again.

Sunday Celebrations

The cluster meetings and the cell group meetings took place on Wednesday nights, and group members continued to attend other churches, principally Saint Andrew's Chorleywood, for Sunday services. However, with the number of converts growing steadily, the need for a Sunday service became apparent. This need was an important marker in the growth of the church.

Eventually, the young people found the stylistic differences between Soul Survivor's monthly celebrations and the Sunday services at other churches too great. They were unable to relate as easily to those churches' service content or style. These larger and more established churches were also made up of older adults from many different social backgrounds, making it difficult for young teens to fit in anywhere.

Also, the distance between Chorleywood and Watford proved to be a problem. With many young people unable to drive, there were too many hurdles for converts who wanted to attend a regular Sunday service.

The initial idea had been to integrate students into local churches for regular worship, teaching and ministry. But we quickly adopted a new strategy: Soul Survivor would provide a regular Sunday service that was relevant to young people and compatible with the Christian culture to which they had been introduced. In 1995, Soul Survivor Watford began to meet on Sunday mornings at a university in Bushey, near Watford.

The Warehouse

We made plans to find a permanent home for our nomadic community. Dreggs was getting more difficult to organize on a regular basis because the venues being rented couldn't be booked all at once and the rental began to prove costly.

After looking at various buildings, we finally succeeded in acquiring a warehouse in North Watford. We financed the acquisition of the warehouse with a mortgage and with interest-free loans and gifts, many of which were from people we didn't even know. We had a budget of £20,000 (approximately $33,000) to refurbish the building. However, the actual cost came to £110,000 (approximately $175,000). Fortunately, we were able to cover the additional cost with interest-free loans and gifts, including a very generous gift from Saint Andrew's Church, which supported us throughout.

Every member of the church felt the excitement. As soon as the deeds were signed on May 31, 1995, we held a prayer meeting in the midst of the dirt and rubble of the unfinished building. Then we ambitiously scheduled a ministry training day for a month later. On the ministry training day, we expected 300 people to attend. Church members worked around the clock to get the warehouse ready. At 4 A.M. the day of the training event, carpet was still being laid in the main church area. At 5 A.M., we vacuumed the carpet and at 10 A.M. that morning, people began to arrive!

Our Accountability Structure

Soul Survivor Watford is part of the Anglican Church. The church is accountable to the Bishop of Hertford. We established explicit support from Saint Andrew's and the diocesan authorities of Watford. As we grew, it was crucial to us that we developed and maintained excellent relationships with the leadership of other local churches as well.

We have been greatly blessed by the pastor of the Anglican Church whose area we share. And Reverend Chris Cottee from Saint Peter's Church agreed to become the chaplain for Soul Survivor Watford. Among other functions, he administers Communion and brings a depth of experience, wisdom and stability that we value very much. Every so often Saint Peter's Church and Soul Survivor Watford meet together for a joint service to maintain friendships and good communication.

Initially, a helpful endorsement came from the Bishop of Hertford who wrote to all the churches in his diocese affirming that Soul Survivor Watford was "a Christian outreach to young people on behalf of the Church of England with close associations with Saint Andrew's Chorleywood. It enjoys the support of the neighboring Anglican parishes in Watford."

Financially, the leadership of Soul Survivor Watford remains accountable to the Church of England through a board of trustees comprised of five Soul Survivor Watford members. All matters of financial protocol are also monitored by the regulations of the Charity Commission in the United Kingdom.

Our Outreach

Time and money previously spent renting venues could now be spent on diversifying our outreach. Having our own property also released new forms of creativity.

Overall, the warehouse opened many opportunities for Soul Survivor Watford. It wasn't long before there were meetings every Sunday morning and evening.

After a two-year hiatus, we relaunched Dreggs at the warehouse in 1997. The basics remained the same, but in our own warehouse we were able to create separate areas in the building: a café with movies, games and pool tables; a dance room with low lights and a DJ. Dreggs carried on as such on an eight-weeks-on, four-weeks-off schedule. We developed a good relationship with a community police officer, who proved to be so supportive he attended the evenings out of uniform in case there was any trouble.

Schools

In 1997, we appointed a schools and community coordinator who was responsible for coordinating activities in the area. This came out of our growing passion to reach the hurting and broken areas of our community by showing the love of Jesus in practical ways. With this new staff person and the facilities at the warehouse, we were able to accomplish much more. We ran lunchtime Bible clubs, a weekly Parents and Tots group and an after-school club for kids aged 7 to 11, which we called Jigsaw. In addition, the schools and community coordinator regularly went to local primary schools to talk and listen to children who were struggling at school.

Pulse

After Soul Survivor Watford had been running at the warehouse for a number of months, we found that Dreggs began attracting young people even younger than 14. We started thinking about how we were going to retain our primary outreach to 14- to 18-year-olds.

In September 1998 we started Pulse, a dance club environment based on the Pulse venue we run each year at the Soul Survivor festival. Gone were the pool tables and videos that attracted the younger people, and out came loud dance music and guest DJs for the 14- to 18-year-olds. The hope and prayer for the event was that meaningful relationships would be made between the young people of Watford in a place that bridged the gap between the school ministry and the Sunday services.

Pulse provided an opportunity to introduce young people to a form of worship to which they could relate. We made relationships with a local security firm called Pulse Security, oddly enough, and they helped keep an eye on things. That allowed the members of Soul Survivor Watford to build relationships, not just police the events. Pulse was open most Friday nights from 8:30 to 11:00 P.M. and was run by Beth Redman and STORM, our resident dance group.

Vision

In the last few years, many changes have been made in the staff who run our initiatives; Jigsaw and Pulse have ended and new initiatives have sprung up in their place. One thing we have come to realize about what we do is that those leaders who have vision for a project are crucial to maintaining and running that project.

Our Teenagers

When we began in September 1993, some members of the core team were still in their teens. Five years later, however, many were getting married and starting families. By 1998, Soul Survivor Watford had over 300 members, 15 cell groups and 2 assistant

pastors who were employed to assist Mike Pilavachi in pastoral responsibilities and care of the church.

Coupled with this was the number of families who had migrated to us. The addition of these families contributed to church stability, by providing nontransient participation and dependable financial contributions. However, with that stability it became important to remind ourselves that primarily we are a missionary congregation to youth. We must continue to develop outreach relevant to the constantly evolving tastes of young people.

Soul Survivor Watford is now a church of over 500 people, with a morning and an evening Sunday service, 18 cell groups and 3 cluster groups. The church has nine full-time staff members including an administrator, a secretary, a youth-outreach worker, a youth pastor, three assistant pastors, one associate pastor and the senior pastor.

Our Current Programs

We continue to live out our values of intimate worship, quality relationships and relevant evangelism through the following programs:

Intimate Worship
- Early morning prayer
- Intercessors
- Nights of prayer
- Musicians and singers evenings
- Creative Vibe (worship through photography, art, sculpture, dance, drama and creative writing)
- Ministry teams
- Pastoral prayer ministry
- Songwriting
- Sunday services

Quality Relationships
- Soccer and basketball nights
- Innit and Xtreme (club nights for young teens and late teens)
- Connect (newcomers group)

- General cell groups
- Cluster meetings
- Church socials (i.e., dances, golf days, paintball, theater trips, house parties)

Relevant Evangelism
- Alpha courses
- Soccer and basketball nights
- Parents and Tots Club
- Area 2 (open youth work)
- Innit and Xtreme (club nights for young teens and late teens)
- Wacky Warehouse (school holiday club)
- Pregnancy Crisis Center
- Schools
- Street life (Saturday night street evangelism team that gives out tea and coffee while chatting and praying with people)
- The Noise (monthly community service event where teams share God's love through car washes, trash cleanup and other service projects)

Sunday Services

We continue to hold two Sunday services, one at 10:30 A.M. and another at 7:00 P.M. We always seek to facilitate relationships by serving breakfast before the morning service, and coffee, sweets and light entertainment after the evening service.

Musical worship is given a high priority in our services, and we try to remain open to the Holy Spirit's leading, giving space for God to speak. Biblical teaching and prayer ministry also take a high priority. Our services remain fairly informal and our deepest desire is to honor God, remain passionate about Him and glorify His name in all that we do.

Cell Groups

Since starting cell groups, we have seen a significant development in our approach. Our church members are free to choose which cell group they attend. Cell group leaders are free to recruit members and we use these leaders as best as we can. We invest time in our cell leaders realizing that a cell group is only as

good as the leader who leads it. We've found that the best way to develop cell groups is to allow them to grow organically.

OUR WORSHIP

Worship has been central to Soul Survivor since its inception. We have experienced a voyage of discovery with many mistakes and painful episodes as we as individuals and as a community have explored a life of dedication to Christ. We found the model of singing intimate songs to God with an acoustic guitar arrangement the most conducive and culturally relevant. However, it has always been about the journey with God more than about musical taste or style.

The Heart of Worship

In the autumn of 1996, we realized that there was something amiss with our worship. At first it was difficult to pinpoint the problem because on the surface everything appeared to be fine. Many of the musicians had learned how to tune their instruments, and the sound engineers were actually getting out of bed on time. Each service contained a block of songs that focused on the Cross and gave people the chance to get down to business with God. To make this easier, the music was up to date, the chairs had been removed and the lights were dimmed.

Yet we seemed to have lost the spark. We noticed that although we were singing the songs, our hearts seemed far from God. Was it Matt Redman's fault? He wasn't singing any more bad notes than usual. Then it clicked. We realized that we had become worship consumers instead of worship participants. In our hearts we were judging the worship time with thoughts such as *Not that song again; I can't even hear the bass;* or *I like the way she sings.* We had made the band the performers of worship and ourselves the audience. We had forgotten that we are all performers in worship and that God is our audience. We had forgotten that sacrifice is central to biblical worship. In the

Old Testament, whenever the people of Israel gathered to worship they sacrificed a lamb or another animal. When King Solomon and the people gathered to dedicate the new temple to the Lord, Solomon sacrificed 22,000 cattle and 120,000 sheep and goats (see 2 Chronicles 7:5). Second Chronicles 7:3 says that the glory of the Lord fell on the people and they fell prostrate on the ground and worshiped. In fact the presence of God was so tangible that for a while even the priests couldn't perform their duties.

We don't need to sacrifice sheep and goats today and certainly no sacrifice on our part can earn God's forgiveness or our own salvation. Jesus' perfect sacrifice has done that for all time. Yet we are called to bring sacrifices in worship. We are called to offer our bodies as living sacrifices because this is our spiritual act of worship (see Romans 12:1). We are called to offer our sacrifice of praise (see Hebrews 13:15).

During worship we needed to ask ourselves, *When I come through the door of the church, what am I bringing as my contribution to the worship?* The truth hit us: Worship is not a spectator sport, and it is not a product molded by the tastes of consumers. It is not about what we can get out of it; instead it's all about God.

We needed to take drastic action. In order to truly learn this lesson, we banned the band. We sacked Redman! Then we sat around in circles and said that if no one brought a sacrifice of praise, we would spend the entire meeting in silence. At the beginning we almost did—it was a very painful process. We slowly learned not to rely on the music. After a while we began to have some very sweet times of worship. We all began to bring prayers, readings, prophecies, thanksgiving, praises and songs. Someone would start a song a cappella, and then everyone would join in. Then someone else would start another song. The excitement came back. We weren't just having church; we were meeting with God. With all the comforts stripped away, we worshiped from the heart.

When we had learned our lesson, we brought the band back. It was at this point that Matt began to sing the song he had written out of this experience. People wept as we sang it for the first time. These words expressed exactly what was going on:

When the music fades,

    All is stripped away, and I simply come,

    Longing just to bring

    Something that's of worth

    That will bless Your heart.

I'll bring You more than a song,

    For a song in itself is not what You have required.

    You search much deeper within,

    Through the way things appear;

    You're looking into my heart.

I'm coming back to the heart of worship,

    And it's all about You,

    All about You Jesus.

    I'm sorry Lord for the thing I've made it,

    When it's all about You,

    All about You Jesus.

King of endless worth

    No one could express

    How much You deserve.

    Though I'm weak and poor

    All I have is Yours, every single breath.[1]

Note

1. Matt Redman, "When the Music Fades," Copyright © 1997 Kingsway's Thankyou Music/MCPS. Used by permission.

Chapter Two

SOUL SURVIVOR
THE MESSAGE 2000

The genius that revealed itself that day could be attributed to the water in the city of Skegness; or, it could be credited to the coffee beans. Regardless of the origin, something extraordinary happened when three men met for coffee in 1997. The vision solidified by Mike Pilavachi, Matt Redman and Andy Hawthorne that day subsequently impacted 12,000 young Christians, and the ripples expanded to affect the lives of many residents in Northern England's largest city, Manchester.

In 1991, evangelist and leader Andy Hawthorne founded the World Wide Message Tribe. This dance music group and ministry, also called The Message to Schools Trust, endeavored to reach young people in the schools of Manchester with the good news in a way the students could understand and relate to. Born and raised in Manchester, Andy loves the city and the young people who call it home.

His driving passion for the teenagers of Manchester led him to challenge Mike Pilavachi and Matt Redman on that windy Skegness morning. Andy urged them to hold the summer 2000 Soul Survivor festivals in the heart of Manchester—not in rural Shepton Mallet as they had for years—for the sake of Manchester.

The idea was radical. The Soul Survivor festivals had been in existence for five years, and already more than 12,000 young people made the annual August pilgrimage to Shepton Mallet for worship, teaching, events and activities. The growth was astounding. Would it be wise to change a tried and true formula? As we considered the possibility, we realized that in order to stay true to the values of Soul Survivor—to enable and empower young people to live radical lives while following Jesus—we had to heed our own words we taught each year at our five-day jamboree: Christian faith isn't just about Christians. Christian faith is about responsibility to God's world and to the people He made for relationship with Himself.

After indulging ourselves in the "what if's" and "wouldn't it be amazing's," it was time for talk to become action. We made the decision: The Soul Survivor festivals would be held in Manchester in the year 2000. By spring of 1998, the Mission to Manchester 2000—or SSM2K as it became known—was gathering steam, and the enormity of the commitment began to sink in. We launched the Manchester initiative in 1998 as preparation for reaching into Manchester with the love that God had extended to us.

THE CAUSE

We immediately realized that we would need the help of other agencies. The Oasis Trust and Youth for Christ (YFC) soon joined hands with Soul Survivor and The Message to Schools Trust (MTST), and the four groups began to plan the biggest urban adventure of our lives.

The festival needed to be an event in which all four of these organizations could utilize their strengths and share resources, ideas, expertise and responsibility. Each agency coordinated the activities at which it was most adept, with as little overlap as possible. MTST had contacts, resources and experience working with the local network of Manchester churches. Oasis brought experience running social-action projects on a local level and handled the practicalities of the service projects. YFC brought their evangelism training programs and small-group expertise. Soul Survivor brought organizational experience, our worship distinctive and 12,000 young people eager to experience Christ and make Him known. The opportunity to work with these fine organizations was a great blessing and encouragement to us all.

Local Churches

The partner agencies took responsibility for the overall event, but there was another key player: the local church. Without the cooperation, unity, prayers and follow-up of the local churches, the lasting impact of the event would be minimal. In March 1998, we conveyed our vision for SSM2K to the churches of Manchester, inviting them to play a critical role in the event. From the start, they understood the vision and made it their own. Soon local churches started meeting together to pray and talk about what they could do to help the project. The network of prayer and support from the local churches became crucial to the vision, playing a pivotal role in the preparation and follow-up of the event. "No more hit and run" became the headline on all SSM2K publicity. We were convinced that whatever God was going to do in Manchester in the summer of 2000, it wouldn't end when the young people left.

Prayer

A vision of this size immediately forces those involved to their knees. One group in Manchester decided to meet every three months, starting in early 1998, to pray for the event. Churches held citywide prayer meetings; and to the amazement of all involved, the meetings drew between 500 to 17,000 people to pray for their city. In Watford, Soul Survivor held nights of prayer; and around the country, God's people joined together to pray for SSM2K.

Framework

Once we established a network of support and prayer, we began to nail down the framework of the event. We decided to have two five-day festivals, with the same program for each festival. We mustered up our creative genius and dubbed the festivals SSM2K-A and SSM2K-B, respectively. Once the dates were set, we began hammering out the content of the five days. We decided on a program that mixed the best parts of a regular Soul Survivor festival with opportunities to reach out to the people of Manchester through the words and actions of Jesus.

THE EVENT

On July 29, 2000, roughly 6,000 young people arrived in Manchester to take part in the first week of SSM2K. These young people came from across the United Kingdom and from nearly every continent, including Australia, North America, South America, Europe and Africa.

After registration, the participants pitched their tents in their designated village areas. Village hosts oversaw each village, making sure things ran smoothly and ensuring that the 50 or so young people in their respective areas were comfortable and well informed. Even though Heaton Park was only used for sleeping, eating and resting in between missions and events, we wanted to make sure that the young people were comfortable and safe, and felt the familiarity of previous festivals. During the day, participants would participate in service projects, outreach and events at Manchester Evening News Arena (MENA), the venue for morning and evening gatherings.

The general outline of a participant's day looked like this:

MORNING	Gather for teaching and worship at the MENA
AFTERNOON	Participants had three options: 1. Build relationships with young people in local cafés 2. Establish contacts with young people throughout the city through First Contact teams 3. Engage in service projects to demonstrate the gospel in action
EVENING	Return to the MENA to talk and sing about God, and to provide an opportunity for those contacted during the day to hear and respond to the good news of Jesus Christ

The buzz before the first morning meeting was palpable. The vision had become a reality and 6,000 young Christians were ready to prove that they were committed to reaching others with the good news of Jesus Christ.

Eventually the transport team managed to persuade everyone to get on the buses and make the first trip of many to the MENA.

Mornings

A key distinction of the Soul Survivor festivals has always been the focus on teaching and worship. The young people at SSM2K—although on a mission to serve—needed some typical festival activities geared exclusively to them. Therefore, the mornings consisted of worship, Bible teaching, feedback and encouraging updates on what had happened on the previous day.

The tide of enthusiasm grew, despite the Manchester rain. Leaders brought fresh teachings from God's Word each morning and many people testified about what God was doing for the people of Manchester through the event participants. Everyone prayed in unity, not only for the impact of the mission, but also for the spiritual health of the city. By 12:30 P.M., we were ready to charge out into the streets to join what God was doing in the area.

Afternoons

The afternoons were our primary time to reach out to the young people of Manchester through actions and an invitation to the Kingdom. We envisioned the afternoon projects as a representation of the outstretched arms of Christ to the city of Manchester. However, the impact on the city surpassed our expectations; the impact on the young people was even greater.

Cafés ran in 23 different locations around the city, from church halls to sports clubs to tents set up in central Manchester. The cafés provided a place where event participants could befriend young people and invite them to the evening meetings. Event participants

also staffed these cafés, serving drinks and prepackaged snacks. Often, participants entertained café patrons with live music and drama.

First Contact teams worked in a variety of contexts and venues, from skate parks and shopping centers to cafés and basketball courts. Two experienced leaders led each of the more than 100 First Contact teams of varying size. These leaders encouraged team members to go beyond small talk with people they met by inviting them to the evening events and arranging to go with them. They also got young people to participate in various sporting events and activities that were hosted by churches and located in the local parks.

Ground Level teams were the heart and soul of the vision for SSM2K. These teams simply presented the gospel through their actions. The 12 area coordinators had worked with local churches, community leaders, youth groups and law-enforcement agencies for months before the event to identify the most appropriate places for the ground level teams to serve the residents of Manchester. On four afternoons each week, teams—as few as 12 people and as many as 750—descended on Manchester neighborhoods to show God's love in action. This was the high point of the mission for many involved. The young people cheerfully cleared rubbish, painted walls and

weeded gardens. The young people's willingness to serve complete strangers overwhelmed the residents of Manchester. Some neighbors talked to each other for the first time in years; others showed their appreciation by providing tea and ice cream to the volunteers.

At these afternoon projects, the dedication of the participants astounded both the team leaders and the citizens of Manchester.

At the end the long days of service, the transport team would collect the event participants from the various neighborhoods and cafés and would transport them to the evening meeting. Hungry, weary and dirty, the young people would arrive at the MENA eager to exchange stories about the day's experiences. The young people were amazed at how much they had gained as a result of their service to others.

Evenings

Being in the largest indoor arena in England surrounded by thousands of people gathered for one reason moved our hearts beyond words. Celebration, joy, laughter and challenge filled the evening meetings. The style and content reflected our desire to make the meetings accessible to outsiders and to proclaim the gospel to this generation. A band— either from Soul Survivor or elsewhere—led everyone in anthems of praise all chosen specifically with non-Christians in mind.

The central gathering of the evening always had two parts. The Soul Survivor team would host the first half, which featured a worship band and an evangelistic talk. After a short break, the World Wide Message Tribe would host the second half, involving other well-known Christian bands such as Delirious? We designed the songs, the message and the style of both parts of the meeting to be accessible to non-Christian young people.

During the first half of the evening renowned English speakers such as Dawn Reynolds or J. John presented gospel messages. The young people received fresh confidence in the power of the good news, and guests heard—often for the first time—the story of Jesus presented in an accessible, dramatic way. They were left with no doubt that Jesus invited a response.

The second half of the evening tended to be more performance oriented, enlisting the talents of many of the country's finest Christian bands, dancers and rappers. Finally, another short talk emphasized the importance of Jesus and His work on the cross.

We gave young people multiple opportunities to respond to Jesus throughout the evening. Those who wanted to say yes to Him or wanted to know more talked with a member of our prayer ministry team. We recorded their names and addresses so that a local church could contact them.

Late Evenings

After the evening meeting at the MENA, the young people headed back to Heaton Park to eat, wash up and rest before the next day. At Heaton Park, the young people had a chance to mix with others and enjoy some of the traditional Soul Survivor favorites: cafés, venues such as Pulse and Chasers, and a marketplace. Tight security made the site safe and comfortable, and the information tent stayed open late to make sure the young people got all the help they needed.

24-Hour Prayer

The event team provided security, human resources, first aid and emergency contacts 24 hours a day, all week long. But the largest support didn't come from us. The young people themselves provided 24-hour prayer support based at a tent in Heaton Park. Young people signed up for slots for prayer and reported to the tent at their designated time. The 3:00 A.M. slot was strangely popular! The success of the project hung on the dedicated prayers of the young people, the partner churches and supporters around the country— before, during and after the mission. Only God will ever fully understand the impact their prayers made.

THE IMPACT

One of the most wonderful and humbling things about serving God is that we can never tally exact or quantifiable results, because the work continues long after the program ends. The prayers, school ministry and the follow-up by local churches continued long after the last meeting. However, God in His grace provided many signs of His saving work during the mission, both in the lives of the event participants and the people of Manchester, right before our eyes. The transformation in the hearts of the young people taking part in the mission and the ongoing ministry in the area churches motivated us to keep pushing on.

By the end of the two weeks, 1,500 young people had made first-time commitments to Jesus. The local churches then began the hard work of following up with each person. The lines of responsibility that we had drawn prior to the mission proved effective.

Testimonies

The following accounts serve as testimony to the amazing work that God did through the various aspects of SSM2K.

Sports Teams

One team leader said,

> I went out to see a group of [event participants] working in a park as a sports team. The afternoon was rainy, and there weren't any young people around. The team was discouraged. The next day, I bumped into the leader and asked him if it had gotten any better. He told me that it had. Apparently, about an hour after I left, a group of young people turned up in the park, and they came along to the evening event. Three of [those young people] made commitments to Christ that night.

Changes

The largest Ground Level initiative was the valley project, which involved more than 750 young people. During the 10 days we worked in Manchester, there were no recorded incidents of crime in a neighborhood accustomed to more than 100 incidents a day. At the end of the 10 days, the police officers who had coordinated the project as well as some of the local residents came to the evening meeting to personally thank the event participants.

The police constable said,

> How do you achieve a zero crime rate for 10 days in one of the country's roughest housing [neighborhoods]? Bring in 1,000 Christian youngsters!

Local Churches

One of the coordinators of the Manchester churches said,

This project has given the churches of Manchester a new lease on life and hope for the future. It has showed them that even the simplest of community activities can open the door into people's lives that they otherwise would never have met, and that there are so many people out there with questions who are just waiting for someone who's willing to talk to them and help them on their journey to find answers.

Another said,

> Together with two other churches in our area, we have jointly employed a full-time youth worker to help us cope with the follow-up to SSM2K! It's brilliant. Before the mission, not one of our churches had any young people in them.

Participants

The young people made their way home having seen and heard the impact God's Spirit made on the people with whom they came in contact. They were excited about the gospel and convinced of its power to save and transform lives.

Time and time again, the young people testified to the privilege of being involved in the work of the Kingdom holistically, proclaiming the gospel to Manchester in words, actions and relationships. They learned the definition of bearing witness to Jesus. SSM2K proved that a whole generation of young Christians is passionate about the gospel, committed to serving people and ready to show the love of Christ through their actions. SSM2K also dissolved, in these young people's minds, the distinction between preaching the gospel and showing the gospel through action.

The mission gave thousands of young people a taste of outreach that we pray will stay with them for the rest of their lives. It gave them a model for witnessing that doesn't require an auditorium, music or a show. SSM2K showed young people that they could serve God in their own community through simple relationships and actions.

One 17-year-old participant named Rob said,

> The fellowship was amazing. I [attend] a school where there are no other Christians, so it was fantastic to worship God with thousands of people the same age as me. Our youth group suddenly discovered that [our] faith is relevant and that following Jesus is exciting. [We] used to sit at the back of the church looking miserable, now [we] are in the front row every Sunday morning with [our] arms raised in worship! I wish some of [our] parents would follow suit.

THE CONCLUSION

- We saw the need to work together, to listen to each other, to contribute while expecting nothing in return and to encourage each other. When separate agendas are put aside and groups unite around a bigger vision, blessings abound.

- We saw the power of action. The afternoon projects allowed the young people to get their hands dirty and provoked a huge reaction. Before the mission began, we thought the evening meetings would be the major evangelistic opportunity. But after listening to the testimonies, we realized that more people had been touched through seeing the kingdom of God in action than through attending the evening events.

- It was unrealistic of us to expect that a mission of this scale—by young people, for young people—could be financed solely by those taking part in it. For a project on this scale, it is important to seek support from various sources.

- We need to constantly think of those who don't know the love of God.

- The support of the local church will make or break the long-term effects of a mission.

Chapter Three

YOUTH CHURCH

The phrase "youth church" is a funny expression really. It's not one we particularly like, as it has probably generated more heat than light. People ask, "What does it mean?" "Can you really have a biblical church that excludes people on account of their age?" "Are you simply talking about a glorified youth group?"

In this section, we will clarify what we mean by youth church and how it relates to the Body of Christ. We'll also give some examples of young congregations that are working within the context of the local church.

The Christian Research Association estimates that in the 1980s the Church of England lost an average of 300 teenagers each week.[1] While the causes of this decline are debatable, the truth is that many more young people are now outside the Church of England than inside it.

We believe that one of the most significant ways for young people to be equipped in the kingdom of God is through new forms of church. In that spirit, the following stories show how some young churches are presenting biblical truth to young people in new ways.

ETERNITY

The Beginning

On January 13, 1995, Mark Meardon launched Eternity out of a small Anglican church near Bracknell in the United Kingdom. God had been preparing the way for the church for many years.

Meardon studied physiology and biochemistry at Southampton University, which offered little experience working with young people. "Looking back, it's strange to think about where I am and what I'm doing now," Meardon said. "A shy [pastor's] kid with uncontrollable hair, God used me at school to see many of my friends become Christians. As I left home to go to university, my heart continued to long for the young people there. After graduation I went to Africa but with a vision for Bracknell. I eagerly returned to see about setting up a youth congregation."[2]

Meanwhile, some members of Saint Michael's Warfield, the small Anglican church near Bracknell, continued to meet and pray for God's initiative among the youth. A team of adults from the church started a quarterly youth service that served existing area youth groups. Young people attended the service, but there was little sense of community because the event was only held four times a year. The leaders learned a lot about running youth services from that first attempt.

When Meardon returned to Bracknell in the autumn of 1994, he wrote to the youth coordinators, highlighting the limitations of the quarterly youth service and suggesting several other options. He also mentioned that he was willing to take a year off from school to pursue the vision of working with young people. Soon after, the team of adults turned all responsibility for the youth service over to Meardon and four volunteers.

The small team began to meet together to pray for God's vision and direction. At one such meeting, they wrote the following mission statement:

> To build a community in which Christians and non-Christians can experience God's love.

They changed the style and format of the youth service to coincide with their mission statement and new name—Eternity. The team led three Sunday evening services in the span of three months. But when the numbers of

youth service members dropped from 120 to 30, the team tried an alternative caroling service in December. "The alternative carol service of December 1994 was the embarrassing last straw of the Sunday services, with songs like 'It Came Upon a Midnight Clear' played to the tune of 'All Along the Watchtower' by Bob Dylan," Meardon said. "Everybody makes mistakes."[3]

After the rise and fall of the Sunday services, the team took a new direction. After much prayer, they began biweekly Friday night services, hoping the increased frequency would nurture a greater sense of community.

"On January 13, and with a budget of £20 [approximately $33], we held our first Friday evening service," Meardon recalled. "There was some worship, a bit of a talk and an appeal. Of the approximately 40 people who came, 7 became Christians. These kids were the first fruits of the ministry. What were we to do with them? We arranged an impromptu follow-up, and the response encouraged us to continue."[4]

Due to growth, the biweekly services became weekly meetings of worship, Bible study and prayer. The growth also forced the formation of cell groups. Initiated and led by young people, the groups appealed to new believers as well as to Christians looking for discipleship. Unfortunately, the young age of the leaders resulted in some growing pains; a number of them really struggled with their roles during this early stage.

The Next Stage

As the congregation grew, it developed a desire to reach out to non-Christians. People regularly brought their non-Christian friends, but the congregation needed a more organized approach. They decided to launch a Drop in Café where kids could hang out, talk, listen to music and drink coffee. Eventually, more young people began to join Eternity through the Café. This initially put a strain on the congregation because the services became more rowdy. People complained that they couldn't worship unhindered while non-Christian kids made noise and heckled during the talk. The leadership of Eternity had to address these issues.

During the next few years, some key changes took place. The café evolved into an under-18 nightclub and moved to the center of Bracknell. Eternity also started a second café in a neighboring town. Sometimes Eternity's leadership altered the services to accommodate the non-Christian young people; other times they geared meetings toward Christians. They developed more structured training for the cell group leaders and offered those leaders more support. They established a team to pursue opportunities in the schools and to assist at the nightclub. The young church also developed a working relationship with the local village government, which led to a joint project pioneered in a local secondary school.

Eternity needed one more key change. The church needed a venue to serve as a base for all the work that was taking place. After we prayed and fasted for a solid week, God blessed Eternity with the use of an old nightclub in the basement of a parking structure where they could stage all the café outreaches and services.

Lessons Learned

Of all the lessons Eternity learned, the most vital is the all-important power of prayer. Sometimes the ministry's growth seemed to depend on the momentum of their latest project. Unfortunately, the young church discovered that this method often resulted

in burnout or complacency. Through many difficult trials, Eternity learned that prayer is the key—relying on God for all we need—whether it be buildings, leaders or money.

Another lesson Eternity learned is the importance of clear vision, values and direction. Since the inception of Eternity, the church's values have been clearly laid out and revisited often. They are

1. Values Toward God
We aim to be worshipers in spirit and truth.

> Yet a time is coming and has now come when the true worshipers will worship the Father in spirit and truth, for they are the kind of worshipers the Father seeks (John 4:23).

2. Values Toward Each Other
We aim to love each other and to express this love by laying down our lives for each other.

> My command is this: Love each other as I have loved you. Greater love has no one than this, that he lay down his life for his friends (John 15:12-13).

3. Values Toward Those Who Are Not Yet Christians
We aim to let God give us a passion for those who don't yet know Jesus so that we can express to them what God has done through Jesus.

> Those who sow in tears will reap with songs of joy. He who goes out weeping, carrying seed to sow, will return with songs of joy, carrying sheaves with him (Psalm 126:5-6).

Having a firm vision and well-defined values allows Eternity to remain highly flexible in all areas of the church. This also allows for quick response to changes and needs.

IGNITE

Simon Jones saw the benefits of youth church firsthand. His first congregation, Awesome, grew from 30 young people to 140 in only 18 months. That experience led him to plant a new Anglican youth church called IGNITE, an experiment in transforming, training and empowering young people. His philosophy is that church should engage culture, involve its youth and be an authentic expression of the people of God.

According to Jones, the following six principles summarize the most important lessons he learned along the way.

1. Have Faith in People

We realized very quickly that chasing trends and cultural relevance were big mistakes. Culture changes so fast, it's impossible to keep up! As soon as you think you've encapsulated culture, it changes again. But that's okay because young people aren't looking solely for snappy trends—they crave involvement. That is the key expression of Church for young people. For IGNITE, it meant taking a risk and allowing the youth to set the agenda in some ways. We had to release the secrets of how to preach, lead worship, pray for healing and run small groups. We realized that a leader's job is not just to do things, but also to get things done. Katy, a 19-year-old student from IGNITE, said,

> I can now contemplate a music ministry course next year. Simon encouraged us to lead worship when we were 13 and 14. Even though we were rubbish, he believed in us. It's given me confidence.[5]

Give away responsibility. *Delegate; don't abdicate!* The impact your young people can have is surprising when you raise your expectations of them. For example, one of our young leaders (age 19) spoke at Awesome.

She said some of the things that I've said a thousand times to the youth congregation! But she communicated the message in a very real way, and it had a tremendous impact. We encourage everybody to get involved in one way or another, so we use our artists, singers, dancers, talkers, musicians and technicians as much as we can. In order to evolve, you have to involve. Involving your young people—and believing in them—is an expression of authenticity, and authenticity mirrors relevance.

2. Practice What You Preach

Keep it real! A young person once told me, "I went to a church recently, and it was like they were speaking a different language!" The Church has an urgent responsibility to demonstrate that faith and real life go hand in hand.

That means we should talk about issues that affect people, including unemployment, bullying and those "What am I going to do with my life?" questions. For instance, if you're going to talk about healing, you must demonstrate how it works! Jesus exemplified this model. He showed the disciples how to pray and stood with them while they tried it—and it's not surprising that they spent the rest of their lives putting it into practice. Give a man a fish and you feed him for a meal; teach a man to fish and you feed him for life.

Jesus was the Word in the flesh, and yet for 2,000 years we've been trying to turn the flesh back into words again! Live out faith; don't just talk about it. Every time we meet on a Sunday night, we expect God to be there, communicating and demonstrating His love for each of us.

3. Cultivate Worship That's Inclusive

We often confuse two things in the Church: style and content. Content is what we do and style is how we do it. We realized that we needed to have prayer at the center of church life. Prayer is one of those nonnegotiable parts of any ministry! But we could develop various styles of praying. Kerry, a 23-year-old, said,

> I feel so embarrassed at the thought of praying out loud and everyone listening.[6]

One Sunday, we wanted to pray for people who had exams coming up. We encouraged everybody to stand and think of something to pray. On a count of three everybody prayed their prayers out loud and in unison. It was noisy, messy, powerful, and guys like Kerry could participate without feeling intimidated by others.

I'm sure you're aware that in nightclubs around the world DJs are leading people. It's a worship-like experience for clubbers—the music moves them as the DJ conducts the masses. So why aren't DJs leading worship in our churches? Why aren't we encouraging these talented young people to worship in a style that is natural for them? After all, didn't the Wesley boys steal the bar tunes of their day and put Christian lyrics to them? We call them hymns now!

We have begun experimenting with DJ-style worship at IGNITE; this type of worship is led by a young guy who has the gifts to make it work. And it can work.

4. Create an Informal Church in an Informal Culture

Do everything you can to help people relax. We use subdued lighting and lots of music,

mixed with plenty of opportunities to mingle. Each Sunday evening we include a "What God's Been Doing" segment. On one of these occasions, a girl named Lesley got up to tell everyone what a painful and difficult time she'd had with a bad back. It was a shocking and honest account of isolation and near devastation. About 10 people identified with her pain and hardship and came to ask Lesley to pray for them afterwards. A 17-year-old named Dave said,

I love to hear people's stories.[7]

Culture seems to be fascinated more with the small story than with the big story. Even advertisements now draw us into the life of an individual in order to sell us a product. Allow people to tell their stories. It sounds obvious, but when was the last time someone in your church got up just to share what a difficult week he or she had? Or that he or she felt like smacking the boss, but God helped him or her hold back? For most young people, honesty is more important than politeness, so release the micronarrative in your church: The small story can make a big impact.

5. Make Disciples

Most companies measure their success based on their size. However, we seek to break the large into the small by practicing a cell-church strategy. At IGNITE, we're trying to encourage, disciple and reach others through a network of small groups. We aim to be a church *in* small groups rather than a church *with* small groups. Evangelism with young people is easier than it's ever been, but discipleship is much more difficult—someone must rise to the challenge.

Cell groups promote intimacy, support and mentoring and encourage the growth of young leadership.

Thus far in our journey, we've seen the following:

- Young people make the decision not to have sex before marriage and then have the courage to explain their decision to their friends at school.

- At an intergenerational church, people of all ages serve one another.

- Painful memories of the past laid to rest.

- Fear of the future replaced by a dependence on God.

- Young people catch the vision of going out to lead and serve in their place of work, in school and in other countries.

6. Face Outward, Not Inward

We cannot sit back, look at the depressing statistics and do nothing. There's urgency in developing new ideas of church within existing structures to try and reach young people.

At IGNITE, each person is encouraged to take responsibility for his or her own network of friendships. We can no longer separate work, play and church. Faith has to hit the ground running in our workplaces and our schools. Therefore, we've tried to equip people to get out into the local community.

Each week we collect a food offering and distribute it to those who need it. Our church members recently spent a weekend picking up litter, painting rooms, cleaning gardens and organizing a community soccer game. At church on Sunday morning, I sent the congregation out to be a sermon by picking up litter from the streets. It had a massive impact on them. The days of sitting with our heads beneath the railing trying to keep a low profile must be over! We're Christians and proud to follow Christ!

We're encouraged by the opportunity given by the bishops of London and Willesden to develop new ideas of church with young people. After all, we want to see the Church go way beyond 2020! To quote Neo from the film *The Matrix*, "I don't know the future. I didn't come here to tell you how this is going to end. I came here to tell you how it's going to begin. Where we go from here is up to you!"[8]

SOUL SURVIVOR HARROW

The story of Soul Survivor Harrow began with the youth ministry of three Anglican churches in Northwest London, known as the Roxeth Team. The ministry the Roxeth Team began in Harrow would undergo a major metamorphosis before it grew into what is now known as Soul Survivor Harrow.

In 1995, the Roxeth Team leaders, Mike and Liz Resch, felt frustrated and disheartened by the lack of young people being equipped by their ministry. Only 12 young people joined the ministry, representing only two of the three churches. Although the events the team put on attracted a large number of young people, most of those young people didn't make the transition to attend regular church, and the few who did soon left.

The Reschs, however, would not be deterred. They felt called by the Lord to minister to young people—whether to 12 or 1,200. They rounded up their handful of young people (6 from St. Peter's Church, West Harrow, and 6 from Christ Church Roxeth) and started Fish with Attitude, a group of young people hoping to connect with Jesus.

At the time, Mike Resch was meeting regularly with Mike Pilavachi. Pilavachi's philosophy made sense, so Resch adopted some of the principles for Fish with Attitude.

Worship

The group craved worship. It was such a high priority for them that, lacking a worship leader, they sang along to worship CDs. This karaoke worship was painful at times, but it offered glimpses of what could happen.

Mike Resch encouraged 1 of the 12 young people, David Gate, to take up playing the guitar. Before long, David began leading worship, though it was awful at first! In those early days he would have to stop strumming to change chords, but to the joy of all, he rapidly improved. Mike and Liz also organized trips to various worship events like Grace in Ealing and Saint James the Less in London.

Relationships

The group also focused on building strong relationships with one another. They spent time hanging out, playing soccer and getting to know each other. They did the kind of stuff that most youth groups do, but they emphasized worshiping God, teaching the Bible and waiting on the Lord. The original 12 young people also built friendships with others and invited those friends to join Fish with Attitude.

As time went on, the Resch house could no longer hold this group of young people. They started to meet in a church hall, while trying to maintain the living-room appeal by decorating the hall with mats, cushions, coffee tables and lamps. However, the group missed the intimacy it had enjoyed before.

In October 1996, Mike Resch took a trip to South Africa where he met with Mark Meardon. After this meeting, Mike felt the Lord drawing him to implement peer-led cell groups at Fish with Attitude. Upon Mike's return home, Liz confirmed this vision, saying that she too felt the same call. The following February, the group divided into four cell groups. Each group met biweekly, and in the off week, all four groups gathered for a single Sunday meeting.

A New Name

As Mike Pilavachi and Mike Resch continued to meet, they discovered that Fish with Attitude shared the same values that Soul Survivor Watford claimed: intimate worship, quality relationships and relevant evangelism. With these close links between the two groups, Fish with Attitude changed its name to Soul Survivor Harrow in March 1997.

Leadership

Initially, Soul Survivor Harrow met every other Sunday evening. However, they soon realized that the cell groups needed to meet weekly rather than biweekly to maintain connection and intimacy. In response to this need, the Reschs released their young people to hold their own evening services, which met in different locations. The risky transition proved worthwhile as Mike and Liz encouraged key young people to move into leadership roles within Soul Survivor Harrow. In time, these young people led services, worship and prayer ministries and took responsibility for the setup and welcome at their services. Then an amazing thing happened—the young leaders started to go back to the morning services in the churches and serve there in addition to serving within Soul Survivor Harrow. After about three months, Soul Survivor Harrow began meeting together, not just in cell groups, on a weekly basis.

Destiny

In addition to developing cell groups and weekly Sunday celebrations, the Reschs and a team from Soul Survivor Harrow started going into schools to teach during lunch. The team also ran an Alpha course at the local college as part of the religious curriculum. These expansions fostered more contacts with young people leading to the need for a place to follow up on those contacts. Soul Survivor Harrow started Destiny as a result. Destiny is a monthly Saturday evening nightclub for young people between the ages of 14 and 18.

It didn't take long for word to get out. In a short time, more than 200 young people attended the club on a regular basis. The nightclub created such a buzz that kids would travel long distances to spend their Saturday evenings at Destiny. Destiny also helped new members of Soul Survivor Harrow get more involved.

Problems

As with any ministry, Destiny had its share of problems. Soul Survivor Harrow leaders weren't oblivious to the dangers of running such an event, so in September 1999 the group employed a local security firm to ensure the safety of the venue. This arrangement worked well, freeing up the leaders and young people of Soul Survivor Harrow to spend time building relationships.

Destiny became a launching point to get young people plugged into other ministries at Soul Survivor Harrow. At first, most of the people who came to the nightclub had no interest in attending a Sunday evening service; but as we built relationships with them, some made the transition to the worship celebration.

Another aspect of the ministry developed because of the deep compassion the young people had for the homeless. Once a month, a team of about 16 young people traveled to London's West End to bless homeless people with sandwiches and soft drinks.

Of course, there have been leadership changes since Soul Survivor Harrow began in 1995, but we are confident that God initiated these changes. The Soul Survivor Harrow congregation now comprises more than 100 young people, and its ministries continue to expand.

Growth

The growth might be due, in part, to the Soul Survivor Harrow leaders, who encourage and release young people into leadership. Because the young people are part of the leadership—investing their own blood, sweat and tears—they have a passion to see the ministries grow. In this model, the adult leaders play a role similar to that of a parent: They guide and educate those in their charge. Sometimes young leaders have to learn the hard way. One of the biggest challenges for adult leaders is to stay one step ahead of the young people, because once the young people catch a vision, their passion will drive them forward without looking back! Allowing the young people to lead is probably one of the most significant lessons Soul Survivor Harrow learned. This model is great for the youth leader as well.

Another contributing factor to the growth of Soul Survivor Harrow is their philosophy of ensuring that young people feel that they belong. That sense of community fosters behavioral and lifestyle changes down the road, which will hopefully lead to belief in the One who can truly change them for life.

YOUTH CHURCH EXPLOSION

According to statistics, the Church today is not as effective in reaching young people as it could be. In fact, the Church is still losing the young people who already come to our churches. But there is hope: Some wonderful ministries have started up around the globe, dedicating themselves to raising up a generation of believers. These ministries are willing to break the traditional mold of church if it means introducing more young people to the saving power of Jesus Christ.

The Church needs to become an organism that reflects the kingdom of God and reaches into the broken and extremely diverse world of young people.

We need new ideas of church that are appropriate for the culture of our day and that will engage the worlds of the young people we are trying to reach. We hope that the stories we've outlined here will inspire you to utilize new, creative ways to reach the young people in your own community.

Notes

1. Christian Research Association, "Reaching and Keeping Teenagers," conducted in 1992.
   http://www.data-archive.ac.uk/search/ indexSearch.asp?ct=xmlSn&q1=4645 (accessed March 30, 2004).
2. Mark Meardon, quoted in Soul Survivor, *A Guide to Youthwork in the Local Church* (Watford, England: Soul Survivor 2001), p. 27.
3. Ibid.
4. Ibid.
5. Katy, quoted in Soul Survivor, *A Guide to Youthwork in the Local Church* (Watford, England: Soul Survivor 2001), p. 29.
6. Kerry, quoted in Soul Survivor, *A Guide to Youthwork in the Local Church* (Watford, England: Soul Survivor 2001), p. 30.
7. Dave, quoted in Soul Survivor, *A Guide to Youthwork in the Local Church* (Watford, England: Soul Survivor 2001), p. 31.
8. *The Matrix*, DVD, directed by Andy and Larry Wachowski (Burbank, CA: Warner Home Video, 1999).

leadership

Note: The following chapters are based on seminars given by Steve Nicholson at Soul Survivor in August 2001. Nicholson is the senior pastor of Evanston Vineyard Church in Illinois.

Chapter Four

DEVELOPING TRUE AUTHORITY IN LEADERSHIP

BRINGING UP LEADERS

One of the reasons I am so optimistic about the future of the Church is that the Bible shows that the fortunes of God's people rise and fall with their leadership. Many of the people I have met in my travels are very focused, very passionate, very intelligent young people who really want to change things because they are dissatisfied with the status quo. They have vision, passion and are determined to go for it.

My honest feeling is that the best days are ahead of us, but that's based on my faith in young people becoming leaders. If they don't take the baton and run, the rest of the Church will go down with them. The fortunes of the Body of Christ rise and fall with its emerging leadership. If leaders fail to emerge now, the Church—and the world—will have to wait until the next generation.

My desire is that you will become the leader you're meant to be, with a passion that will last for the rest of your life.

FINDING YOUR CALLING

I get excited when young people tell me that God's calling them to be a pastor, a church planter or a counselor. You can't decide to wait until later to start reaching out. Your ministry starts now. It's not about how much you get paid; having a salary doesn't mean your job is more important than someone else's ministry. Finding your calling is about the kind of person you are and the vision that you have, which means you can begin your ministry immediately. Leaders such as Bill Bright, Billy Graham and others began their ministries while they were still young. Many people told them, "You're not ready. You don't know enough." Still, they went ahead and did it.

It's important for you to remember that you won't fully blossom as a leader until you are around my age (I'm in my late 40s). For some of you, that seems like a long time to wait, but that's when things get exciting; that's when your opportunities to influence people will exceed your expectations. That means you've got to make it until you're that age. A lot of people with whom I started leading—people who had a lot of passion and gifting—didn't make it. Some simply washed out somewhere along the way; others crashed and burned horrifically. Whatever the cause, we've lost something by their absence. The following thoughts about leadership will help you remain in the race until you reach the goal of achieving the full measure of what God has for you.

BUILDING YOUR CHARACTER

In talking about leadership, there's only one place to start: your character. Your main project for the rest of your life is yourself. Ultimately, long-term leadership is based on who you are. Think of the person who has influenced you the most over the course of your life. How much of that person's influence is due to his or her character or personality? Chances are, that person practiced integrity, and the same must be true of you if you are to have the same influence on others. So what does integrity look like?

Keep Your Word

Leaders follow up on what they say. If circumstances prevent them from doing so, leaders make sure they notify someone as soon as possible or apologize to the people they have wronged. Reliability is a very serious issue in leadership. If people in your church, ministry or youth group never know if you'll be on time, for example, they won't know if they can trust you with more authority.

Speak the Truth

Would you trust a leader who shades and exaggerates things all the time? Have you ever known someone who rarely says what they mean? Chances are, you'd prefer to follow a person who simply speaks the truth. One of our goals as leaders is to learn how to speak the truth. The problem is that, sometimes, telling the truth hurts. Although it can put us in difficult situations, truthfulness is a critical component of integrity.

Notice how closely integrity is tied to what we say. The integrity of a leader's words lend authority to his or her leadership. Since your words directly affect your authority, you must surrender control over your mouth to God. Simply put, the more you submit your words to God, the more authority your words will have.

Admit Your Mistakes

Another aspect of integrity is admitting your mistakes. Many leaders fear that if they humble themselves in this way, people will not follow them, thus threatening their leadership. Nothing could be further from the truth. When a man or woman says, "I was wrong," the trust of their followers will actually increase. So often I have watched leaders struggle to justify their mistakes. They invent reasons, excuses or words from God; but when it comes down to it, they simply made a mistake. Instead of spending so much time trying to explain mistakes, it would be easier just to say "You know what? I goofed."

Recently I introduced a couple to the congregation to present a new ministry that they would be leading in our church. Now you may have experienced a time when your brain didn't work the way it should and you forgot something important onstage. It was one of those times for me that Sunday morning. When the time came, I introduced the husband and forgot to introduce his wife. They let me know about it soon after! "Is she a part of this ministry or not? Were you trying to tell us something? Are you looking at this differently than we are?"

I replied, "No, I just goofed. I made a mistake; I should have said her name. I will do better next time, and I'll make sure people know she's a part of the ministry. My brain just fritted out." Those simple and humbling words solved the problem.

Another time I was teaching a small-group leader's class. Near the end of the class, somebody asked me how they should handle the theological students who take people off into esoteric theological discussions. I gave a flippant answer that was negative toward seminarians, and as soon as it left my mouth I thought, *I'll get into trouble for that.* Sure enough, that week one of my seminarians said, "You know, I felt really angry when you said that—that really hurt."

I told him that I deserved his anger, that it was a stupid comment and that I shouldn't have said it. I couldn't even believe I had made the comment; it was simply thoughtless and uncaring, and I apologized.

He responded with, "Great! I'm with you 100 percent of the way. I love the way you apologize. You just taught me something more about leadership."

We get along fine now. In fact, he became more committed to me after that incident than before. Why? Because instead of trying to justify my comment, I just said, "Hey, I messed up."

One of the reasons I'm so passionate about this point is that it took me way too long to learn it. I wasted about 10 years dodging, squirming and trying to get through life without having to admit my mistakes. Let me spare you the trouble. When you make a mistake, admit it and then move on. If you become that kind of person from the start, you will be way ahead in issues of integrity.

Get Straight on the Issues of Money and Sex

It's that simple. Both of these issues are problematic in their ability to compromise or confuse us. Money and sex are gifts from God, but they each have a specific and limited place in our lives. It is best to set safe boundaries that eliminate all questions about your character. Put yourself in a place that protects you from the slightest accusation. Don't kid yourself, because even if you stay on the right track, a questionable situation could destroy your ministry. For this reason, speakers such as Billy Graham never stay or travel alone. Billy Graham won't even walk into his hotel room by himself. True accountability like that leaves no room for questions.

Billy Graham takes an average pastor's salary, and everybody knows how much he makes. He doesn't have any special funds on the side, nor does he use the money that God gives him to do ministry for his personal needs. Again, there's no room for questions.

For better or worse, the world cares more about your financial purity than it does about your sexual purity. If you take a big cut of the contributions and use them for yourself, you will surely lose your integrity, influence and authority. If you want to lead a church, particularly in full-time ministry, understand this now: You won't get rich. No matter how big the crowds, you should always strive to live a simple life. This will do away with any possible questions or accusations.

Fight Until the End

Integrity also means that you are committed to working until God tells you to stop. That may mean you'll be there until you're 25, 45, or 65 years of age. But as I stated earlier, that's just when it starts getting good!

Cultivate Security, Humility and Fear

Another aspect of integrity is learning to gain godly security in your life, as opposed to insecurity. One of the biggest struggles for middle-aged leaders is insecurity. This insecurity can drive them to become controlling, manipulative and ineffective in their leadership. Cultivating the self-confidence that stems from knowing yourself and knowing God will help young leaders avoid these pitfalls. It is crucial to know yourself. Deal with issues from your past, such as family problems, abuse or other things that could prove problematic in the future. Do whatever needs to be done to work through those things right away.

Let God reveal those issues or wounds in your life. As He does the work, listen to Him. Your actions are unshakably founded on your relationship with God and His call on your life. Make sure your identity is securely founded in the untouchable fact that first and foremost you are a child of God. It is your relationship with God—not your leadership position—that gives you self-worth. Only then can you become a leader who releases others into leadership, is happy to see people succeed and isn't afraid of losing his or her position. This will make a huge difference in what you are able to accomplish.

Using a leadership position to feed your personal insecurity is a deadly path. Your leadership will become twisted. Like Aaron in the Bible, insecurity will lead you to be influenced by people out of fear. Aaron's fear of the Israelites stemmed from his insecurities in his relationship with God; as a result, he led people into idolatry. When I pray, I don't start out with my ministry or even my church. I start with myself. I stop being a leader and start by putting my relationship with God in place. Only when Steve Nicholson, as a son of

God, is straight with his Father, can he go on and pray for the ministry and the church.

Working hard at your relationship with God will build deep security within you. You will stop looking over your shoulder, wondering what will happen, fretting over who will take your job. You won't have to lead in fear of what people think of you. You will be clear with God.

Someone once asked me what I do when somebody tries to undermine my ministry. I told them that I just laugh because it is nothing. I don't challenge them with questions such as, "What did you say about me?" or statements like, "You shouldn't be saying that stuff! I am the Lord's anointed!" Admonishing people to submit to you inherently disproves your leadership. You might as well quit. If you are truly their leader, you will never need to say it because you will simply lead, and they will follow.

Only one person can take my ministry away: the guy in the mirror. If I mess up and lose my integrity, I will probably lose my ministry as well. No one else can take it from me because it came from God. God called me to this ministry, and I'm here until He moves me elsewhere. (He has my resignation on file, of course. I have already told God that He can move me whenever He wants to, and I usually reissue the statement on Monday mornings.) Though people can take away titles and positions, again, only I can ruin the ministry I lead. You would do well to understand that truth and become secure in that knowledge.

Fear of pride often causes us to miss moving into godly self-confidence. We hide and minimize our gifts, afraid that others will misconstrue our efforts as arrogant. The result is that we feel like we're not competent enough to do anything. But make no mistake, your gifts are from God. In the parable of the talents (see Matthew 25:14-30), Jesus makes it clear that true humility is not burying your talents in the ground. Hiding, minimizing or hesitating to use the gifts God has given you is false humility, and God hates it.

Instead of hiding your gifts and strengths, make the most of them. Don't hold back for fear of making yourself too visible or appearing too proud. Instead, speak the vision you believe God has given you. That is not too ambitious. But while you continue to pursue and use your gifts, you must be able to admit weaknesses and errors. That is the essence of true humility.

Rid your life of guilt and fear, which undermine security. The Bible calls fear of man a snare (see Proverbs 29:25). The fear of what a friend, parent or pastor might say plagues us. Jesus says, "Do not be afraid of those who kill the body but cannot kill the soul. Rather, be afraid of the One who can destroy both soul and body in hell" (Matthew 10:28).

Exchange the fear of man for a fear much greater. Do you think that facing a human authority figure is a problem? Just imagine facing almighty God when He says, "You wasted that gift that I gave you. I prepared this great thing, but because you were afraid of that person, you never did it." Rid your life of that fear by using your gifts.

Fifteen years ago, I experienced the power of God in an awesome way. It felt as if electricity was running through my body and elephants were jumping up and down on my chest. The feeling started suddenly and completely took over, coming in waves. My body wasn't outwardly shaking, but my skin quivered up and down my body, and I could feel the shaking in my bones. I felt like I was going to die—I could hardly breathe. I heard someone screaming, and finally realized that the noise was coming from my own mouth. I felt as though I was lying next to a burning bush and the fire was burning me. I knew I was in the midst of the glory of God. There are so many things God could have gone after in that moment, so many faults and sins; but of all those things, He was really upset about my fear of what other people thought about me. He was after my fear issues, and apparently, He was really ticked. I was alone with God, cooking there for three hours. I didn't care what was going on around me because God was after my fear.

The best way to cure fear is to face fear. As I finished secondary school, I was really on fire for Jesus. The most difficult task I foresaw was telling all the people with whom I'd spent my life (while not being on fire for Jesus) that I had given my life to Jesus. I thought their expectations of me had already been determined. When I went to university soon after that, I knew I had to be free of my fear of what others thought of me. So I bought the biggest leather cross I could find and wore it every day. In those days, the early 70s, little round pin-on political buttons promoting various causes were very popular. So I bought six or seven Jesus buttons and put them on my jackets and backpack. I went school that first day wearing my cross and buttons, and introduced myself with, "Hi, my name is Steve and I'm a Jesus freak." After that I was free to be who I wanted to be, and the other students respected me.

I'm not suggesting you hit the vintage stores for old Jesus pins, but the principle is that you address your fears. Face your fears and you will be fine.

ENCOURAGING GIFTS

Consider the things you have enjoyed doing or have done well in the past. You may want

to seek help from your friends for this task. This is a good starting point, but it is not enough. More than likely, not all your gifts have emerged yet, especially if you're young.

Sometimes you can find out what gifts you have through prophetic ministry. One of the goals of prophecy is to release gifts within the Church. If you have a strong gift in a particular area, people with the gift of prophecy will likely inform you of it more than once. Many people who exercise the gift of prophecy say that it is as if you are carrying a huge sign above your head with your gift written across it.

Sometimes the only way to discover your gifts is to try things—it's like shopping for a new set of clothes. You may have to try on a bunch of clothes before you find what fits. I believe that God gives us a desire for the things with which He has gifted us. Whatever talents God gave you, you probably enjoy using them. Those things you really enjoy doing are likely gifts that He's already put in you.

Sometimes your gifts become apparent through small, hardly noticeable things. For example, someone with a prophetic gift may seem to know things about people. He or she may consider it simple intuition, but it may be an undeveloped gift of prophecy.

It is important not to confuse gifts with roles. A pastoral gift does not mean you will become a senior pastor of a church. Most churches have a lot of pastors, including people who disciple others while still holding a secular job. If someone says you have a pastoral gift, that isn't necessarily a prediction of your future career. It is simply one of your gifts. Chances are, you have more than one gift and confusing those gifts with a precise role could tie you in emotional knots.

Get Experience and Use it

It's a simple fomula: get experience and use it. Somebody once asked me how to recognize what words are from God when developing a gift of prophecy. "I have a sure-fire method for finding out what is from God," I replied. "If it's in line with the Bible, speak it out and we'll see if it's from God by the results."

The person didn't really like that answer, but it's the truth. Sometimes you have to do things that you're not 100 percent sure are

from God. You have to try some stuff. You have to get out there and fall flat on your face. You might risk a little humiliation, but that won't kill you.

Stretch yourself to experience more. If you are currently working in a role that has become easy for you, maybe it's time to take another role. I believe that at a young age you should always be a little scared, feeling as if you don't really know how to do what you are doing. If you're ever around me and I get the impression that you're not a little scared or unsure, I'll do my best to help you get there. I believe that those who feel out of their element—lacking in either knowledge or ability—are those who grow the most. When there is trouble or when you have to do something you've never done before, you'll grow. Those who are comfortable don't grow much at all.

I train pastors, and this year I have five new interns. The first step in the process is for them to lead small groups over a nine-month period. I want them to lead a group long enough to deal with a really messy pastoral situation in which a group member gets him- or herself into trouble, or people start to complain or criticize. That's my plan for them because I know that learning begins when trouble comes. I want them to grow. I want them to gain wisdom. But wisdom is not gained through being comfortable. Wisdom is developed in the heat of desperation.

Leadership is about taking risks. If there is one problem in the Church, it is the lack of risk taking. Mike Pilavachi undertook a wonderful risk in The Message 2000 event in Manchester. You have read about the outcome of that risk. Take those risks and stretch your gifts because you can go so much further than you think.

Find a Mentor

Approaching a more experienced person who has a heart to see others succeed and a gift similar to your own is one of the best ways to grow. If you can, find such a person and follow him or her everywhere.

To be honest, there's a lack of good mentors. Whether you are young or old, there is always someone with less experience than you—become a mentor! You can train leaders, teach leaders and have a great time while you're doing it. It's far more fun to mentor somebody and see him or her succeed than it is to succeed yourself.

One of the young teenagers in our church—a brash and arrogant kid—was graduating from high school as president of his class. He had to give a speech at the graduation ceremony, so we sat down a couple times after church to discuss it. I asked him what he was going to say, and he said he wanted to work his faith into his speech. We discussed several methods for doing this and then went over some ideas for his speech.

Five thousand people were present at the ceremony. This 18-year-old kid spoke for 10 minutes to a crowd that largely comprised nonbelievers and he hit a home run. People laughed, cheered, screamed and clapped—it was awesome. All the other kids gave typical sleepy ceremony speeches, but his was absolutely hot. I tell you I left higher than a kite. It was more fun to listen to him than it would have been to talk to all those people myself. It was wonderful just to see him succeed. I heard people say, "Man, that guy's a Christian; he should be a preacher!"

So find someone to mentor! Hang around them as much as you can. If you know someone who would make a good mentor, don't be bashful. Be a pest! Be forward even if it isn't considered proper! Sometimes all people need is a little push to get them started. (As a side note, thanks to e-mail you no longer have to be present to mentor.)

Study the characteristics surrounding your gifts. You need to read about them and find out everything you can about them. Do your homework! Ask lots of questions. Every time you see somebody using a gift you want to develop, question him or her as to the actions and workings of that gift.

CULTIVATING INFLUENCE

Influencing others is fundamental to your ministry. That means you must develop trust so that people will follow you. You must love and listen to people, be an example to them and be willing to sacrifice for them. Simply being there for someone at a critical moment carries tremendous power.

This kind of investment isn't as costly as it seems. In fact, loving others can be a very simple thing for leaders. As people arrive at a group meeting, take a few extra seconds to ask how their week is going and let them tell you a little about it. It's as simple as that. It costs you nothing, yet they will walk away knowing that their leader cares about their emotional well-being and about them as a person. It communicates love. They see that you have been watching out for them, that you have been thinking about their welfare.

Your own convictions can also be highly influential. If you feel strongly about something, your passion will be magnetic. To be a leader, you need to be on fire for something you really want to accomplish.

Your convictions are related to your vision, but accomplishing the latter requires commitment on the part of your volunteers too. To lead people, you must announce new plans and ideas and challenge your volunteers to do things they never thought they could do. Then you must ask them to commit to seeing the vision completed, or it will never get off the ground.

Growing as a leader requires that you work with a wider team of people. Nothing is impossible for a person who doesn't have to do it himself or herself. If you operate alone, you might draw a crowd, but it will be a small crowd. Working with a team means learning how to lead other leaders. By learning to lead people who, in turn, lead teams of people, you will end up leading a dynamic movement that changes the world around it.

Q & A

Question: I find trying things I'm not sure are from the Lord to be really uncomfortable. How can I be sure of what God wants me to do?

Steve Nicholson: No one wants to do something that is not from the Lord. But my feeling is that it is better to try than not try. Read the parable of the talents again. The guy who buried his talent did so because he was afraid of failing and that was not the right thing to do.

Q: What's the difference between challenging people and controlling them?

SN: You must challenge people to do something they already want to do. There is a place for loving confrontation if you already have a good relationship built on trust. To challenge people is more to encourage them than to confront them.

It's best to say things like, "You can do it!" "Go for it!" "You really need to do this, and I really think you can do it." You're asking them to do something that they want to do, but are afraid to do. Conversely, you control people when you attempt to stop them from doing what they really want to do or when you get them to do something they really don't want to do. Therein lies the difference.

Q: How do you balance reaching out to nonbelievers while remaining fully employed in ministry?

SN: This is a common problem among those involved in ministry. To combat it, you must have a life outside of the ministry. Join a sports team. Have a hobby that allows you to rub shoulders and make friends with non-Christians. Then you will come into contact with the lost and keep your feet on the ground. It will come naturally. If your life is all locked up in your church, you'll end up spiritually deformed, so lead a balanced life.

Q: What do you do when you're not sure what God wants you to do? What if you know that God has called you, but you don't know what the next step is?

SN: Start with what you know and get involved. No boat can be steered in a dry dock, so get in the water and start rowing; God will steer you. He will not let you miss His will. If you are a little dense, He will have every prophet in town barking up your tree. I have even seen God speak through non-Christians to get the message across. You cannot unintentionally miss the will of God. The only way you can miss His will is to look at it, know what it is and say no. Even then it is hard to get away—ask Jonah. Whatever you do, don't just sit there; get involved and do something.

Q: Do you have any other guidelines for accountability, other than having accountability partners?

SN: Accountability does not mean anything if you aren't open and vulnerable with the people to whom you're accountable. Many of those who've ended up in moral failure had relationships for the purpose of accountability, but they didn't reveal anything. The friendships can become nice and convenient, but you neglect to mention all the relevant details of your life. These are insignificant relationships because accountability is only as good as you make it. If you want to be held accountable, you must be prepared to tell someone else about the ugly stuff in your life. Without honesty, accountability can't exist. In the end, whether you stand or fall is up to you. How vulnerable are you willing to be?

Q: Do you think you ever know when you're ready, or do you just go for it?

SN: When you think you're ready, it's already too late. My experience is that when I finally think I understand a job and know what I'm doing, God changes it or raises the stakes. He wants you to walk by faith. He wants you to be in a place where you cry out to him, "O Lord, help!" That is where all the fun stuff happens. So just go for it.

Q: What if you want to go for it, but other leaders say that it's not God's timing for your life? If people tell us to wait and wait, we can become frustrated.

SN: Usually in those conversations, the focus is on leadership as a title or position. You may say, "I want you to give me something," and they reply that it is not God's time yet. If that's what you mean, you're looking at the issue upside down. *Be* a leader. Just start *being* a leader. Be a leader of integrity and reliability. Be a servant. Just start influencing people for God. Nobody can control what you are. They can make you wait for the title, but producing the goods of leadership will entitle you to be called a leader whether you have the title or not. Bottom line, if you need the title, then maybe you aren't a leader. If you really are one, you can't avoid it. Talk to people. If they won't give you a title or a particular position in your church, you can always be a leader elsewhere—anywhere, in fact! Go out into the neighborhood and start leading. Go to the prison and start preaching. You don't need to fit the church's box—your heart is all that is necessary. Nothing can stop it once it's fired up! A lady once told me, "I want to go plant a church." Back then the Vineyard didn't permit women to plant churches or to be senior pastors. I replied, "Look, you go plant a church and trust me, they will find a way to legitimize it! If you start a group of one hundred, you will be recognized as a leader, with or without the title." Stay on good terms with your church leaders. If they advise you to wait, ask them why. Maybe they think you have a character issue that needs work. Graciously accept their comments and humbly work on those areas.

Q: Don't you think that you have to be careful? I mean, if you do things too quickly, or if you are inexperienced and too enthusiastic, couldn't you do an awful lot of damage?

SN: I did a lot of things too quickly and without much experience. I led my church for 10 years without knowing a thing. I took them down a couple of dead ends and hurt a lot of people along the way. However, I believe that this course of action was better than not doing anything at all. Waiting until you have all the answers or until you think you have enough wisdom is far worse than making a few mistakes, because we never stop learning. Wisdom is gained through experience; if you never get out there and try things, you'll never learn. You'll never have all the answers, and you'll never stop gaining new wisdom, so don't make the biggest mistake, which is ignoring God's call. The risk takers aren't hurting the Church—it's those who are too afraid to step out on their own that discourage others from doing so. I tell those who say, "I'm afraid I'm going to make mistakes," that they probably will. That's not a bad thing, but you must learn from your mistakes. You would have to work hard to make more mistakes than me, but I came out alive, and the church came out alive; and though there are a few injured bodies along the way, we're all the better for the journey.

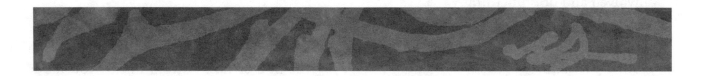

Chapter Five

TURNING VISION INTO REALITY

Once, in a meeting, we were asked, "If you were absolutely certain that you could not fail, what would you like to do? Not in the sense of waving a magic wand to end world hunger, but a realistic desire in your heart that you could potentially do for the kingdom of God."

Some of the answers included

- Build a homeless shelter in California

- Provide more medicine to Mexico

- Plant a church in every nightclub or bar in a particular city

- Unify the Church in a particular place

Knowing that every individual has a true vision, let's identify several steps that will turn that vision into reality. The following steps will help you accomplish the vision God has placed in your heart.

STEPS TO VISIONARY LEADERSHIP

Godly Vision

The vision God gives you will always be too big for you to accomplish on your own. When you accomplish something that you could not have done by yourself, it is a testimony to God's power. He wants us to live a life beyond human explanation, through which He will be truly glorified.

If the vision beating in your heart seems too big or too much for you, that doesn't mean it isn't from God. In fact, if it is too safe, too predictable or too controllable, it probably isn't from God, because the supernatural element is an essential ingredient in godly vision.

As your vision begins to materialize, there are four things to look out for.

1. Borrowed Vision

Be careful not to adopt a vision God has given to someone else. You could easily catch a vision that belongs to a compelling, likable or charismatic teacher. If you admire them and want to be what they are, you may simply be seeking the attention without being aware of the consequences.

Someone may have pressed the vision on you, possibly through parental expectations. However, the origin of such a vision is external. It's not from your heart, which is where God births vision. The problem is that passionate people with strong visions easily influence others. My vision is hundreds of church plants all over the world. I'm a maniac about it and I talk to everyone about it all the time. Sometimes it's hard for people to hang on to their own vision around me.

The key to making sure your vision is your own is to tell the Lord, "I want your will, I want to do something meaningful for you, and I want to serve you." A great sign that the desire is from God is if it consumes your mind on a dreary Monday morning and after a great meeting, festival or conference.

2. Your Abilities

Generally, visions from God have some connection to your past experience or abilities. For example, my vision for church planting may be connected to the different types of clubs and activities I started in school. And my vision for speaking may have something to do with the public speaking I did as a child. The gifts displayed earlier in my life are connected to my present vision. Of course, God is big enough to work without continuity. He may want to develop a new ability in your life.

3. Advice from Others

God often uses other believers to help confirm His will and accordingly strengthen, affirm and encourage the desires of our hearts. He may use your pastoral leaders or even an individual's gift of prophecy to confirm whether your vision is reasonable or appropriate to pursue.

4. Lack of Ego

Be wary about falling into something because it's popular. There is a certain part of almost every human being born after 1960 that wants to play an instrument and be a rock-and-roll star. That isn't God's plan—it's simply a childhood fantasy. If that really is God's plan for your life, you will possess the required abilities. Plus, your vision should connect with who you are as a person.

Faith

To fulfill a vision does not require faith in what you can do but faith in what God can do. Believe in what He can do through people; He loves to do the unexpected, and He likes to move us beyond our comfort zones. Faith always entails risk, and following your vision is no exception. Be reconciled with that fact. Face your fears and dare to find yourself in a place of uncertain success.

In an ideal world, everyone would get an ironclad guarantee of success before starting anything, but there's no faith involved in that. God won't give you immediate results because learning to live by faith is crucial to our development as believers. We need to learn to press on in spite of what's going on around us.

If you fear failure or what others think, allow God to help you press through to victory over those things. If you don't, those fears will keep you from starting—let alone fulfilling—your vision. If you don't stretch yourself to undertake a vision that seems beyond you, you will never achieve your full potential. If you don't strive to use 100 percent of your potential, you will probably never utilize one-tenth of it.

Taking a dangerous walk of faith ensures that, at the end of your life, you will know you made the most of every gift and talent God gave you, and that your fears and insecurities did not paralyze you. Don't allow yourself to have any regrets in life.

Obedience

Faith always leads us to obedience. When God leads, obey! Obedience is having a greater fear of the Lord than of failure. You must be more afraid of disobeying the Lord than of coming up against obstacles.

Look at the story of Noah. God gave him a crazy vision to build a huge boat because the earth would soon be flooded. It must have been hard for Noah to stay obedient some of those days as he sat atop this huge ship, hammering nails, swatting flies, wiping the sweat from his eyes and listening to the neighbors laugh. I'm sure there were days when he just wanted to give up. But he obeyed God, and it's a good thing too, because one day the clouds began to fill the horizon.

Not only do you have to be obedient to the heavenly vision that God has given you, but you must also do it God's way. It is important that you do not make up your own way to fulfil the vision. If Noah had decided to build a skate park instead of an ark, none of us would be here now. Unless you fulfill in His way the vision God has given you, your toil is in vain (see Psalm 127:1).

Powerful Prayer

Pray for each specific piece of your vision. We probably would like to pray the entire vision into being all at once; however, a vision comes together in phases. We must pray for every small piece: the volunteers for the event, the money for supplies for next week's meeting or the location of a gathering place. You must pray for every piece of your vision with equal fervency and passion.

Prayer for healing can be similar. A woman in our church returned from a John Wimber conference to tell me that she saw a man in a wheelchair get up and walk. Noticing my surprise, she looked at me and said, "It wasn't the way you think."

I asked her what she meant and she replied, "This man had been in a wheelchair for a long time. There were no muscles in his legs."

Now during long-term disability muscles deteriorate. A limb eventually becomes just skin over bones. Walking involves muscles from your neck to your toes. She described how the leaders at the conference prayed for the man's muscles one by one. They got him to stand up, discovered where the weak spots were and prayed for each one consecutively. In the same way, you need to pray over each part of your vision. Do you need help, money or wisdom? Be prepared to pray for every single part, however small.

Of course, this means you will spend a lot of time facedown in front of God. Sometimes all you can do is cry out to God because there are no words. I have found that an effective method is to lie on the ground and yell, "Help! This was your idea after all! If you want me to do this, provide what I need to do it!" Let your prayers to God be transparent as you pray your vision into reality.

Discipline

Football coach Vince Lombardi said, "Leaders aren't born, they are made. And they are made just like anything else, through hard work. And that's the price we'll have to pay to achieve that goal, or any goal."[1] To help you be all that you want to be, God has set some tasks for you that you might not necessarily want to do.

It can be difficult to keep spiritual disciplines, such as daily Bible reading, focused prayer time, fasting and serving people, in your life. Don't neglect these disciplines.

ACTION STEPS

Connections

Join a group with similar vision and values. If your vision is to start a homeless shelter, make friends with someone who has experience starting homeless shelters. If your vision is to plant churches, get connected with people who have already planted churches. If your vision is to minister abroad, find someone who is going to the same place and who shares your vision. Making these friends and connections means not having to start everything from scratch and allows for reinforcement, encouragement and help along the way. When you hit a rough spot, you can always talk to those more experienced than you.

When I was 23, I started a church independently and quite by accident. I started with the idea of a worship time I could actually enjoy. As it happened, other people wanted the same thing. As a church, we spent nine years unaffiliated with any larger network until we connected with the Vineyard Church.

I know that if the Vineyard ceased to exist, I could never return to being on my own. I would join another network no matter what. Those nine years of isolation tremendously reduced my ability to fulfill my vision and prevented me from reaching my full potential. Most of the time, I felt as though I was banging my head against a wall. When I connected with others pulling in the same direction, I truly began to see my dreams fulfilled. This connectedness was vital for my ministry.

I believe that anyone God calls to do a significant work is simultaneously called into a community of allies and friends who help fulfill that vision. Each of those people needs to find his or her place in your team of visionaries as he or she works with you.

The only way to build your team is to tell people about your vision. I once spoke at a conference at which an individual had a vision to start a church in every bar. Every chance he gets, he should speak up and tell people, "Hey,

I think we could do something interesting by starting churches in bars and pubs."

Look for people who understand your vision and who will say, "That's what I've always wanted to do! Can I do it with you?"

People who respond this way are already prepared and motivated; all they lack is a leader to take the initiative and provide direction. For every leader there are followers—usually at least 10 to 12 with the skills or abilities you lack—who cannot lead but who want to see the vision realized.

You will probably have to share your vision with 10 times as many people as you need on your team. If your vision is really big, you may need to contact 100 people in order to reach 1. For a large vision, plan on talking to between 100 and 1,000 people in order to build a team of 10 visionaries.

In order to transfer your fire to others, you must express your vision in a tangible way. People must see, taste and touch the significance of the vision in order to decide whether it will be worth the sacrifice. Forget creating a great big fat notebook that presents a nice plan for people to take home and read. A medium such as that may contain a *plan* but rarely any *vision*. A vision should be able to be communicated succinctly, off the top of your head and in any location.

The goal of sharing your vision is to find your "mighty men." First Chronicles chapters 11 and 12 reveal one of the key factors in David's success as a leader. Mighty men of valor came to David's aid while he was in Ziklag, banished from Saul (see 1 Chronicles 12:1). They helped him in battle and "gave his kingship strong support to extend it over the whole land, as the LORD had promised" (1 Chronicles 11:10). A great deal of David's success stemmed from the work God did through these men. As you look to achieve your vision, you also need to look for mighty men and women who will help you fight the obstacles impeding your vision and who will support your leadership.

Generally, you'll want to find people with a variety of gifts. Make a list of the positions needed, such as worship leader, evangelist or teacher. Then ask God to fill the roles you've identified with specific names.

Although these people might be your friends, it's usually better that they aren't. Your friends are probably very capable, but unless they share a passion for your vision, they may not be willing to carry it to fruition. They will likely consent to accompany you because you are their friend, but later they may realize—once the vision is launched and the hardships come—that they don't have the necessary drive or gifts. Without the gifts needed for the job at hand, they may become frustrated. Then you will become frustrated and you might end up with one fewer friend. So leave your friends at home, and they will remain your friends. Let them pray for you and provide resources, but leave them off the team unless they can truly carry out the necessary functions.

Resources

As you embark on your journey, you will likely join the ranks of vision casters who need two resources: time and money. Let's look at money first.

There are many ways to raise money for ministry, but you will have to think creatively. Often, the need for money comes a bit further down the road since, initially, other resources such as people are so desperately needed.

The need for money is not synonymous with vision. I didn't use a dime to plant my first church, and I didn't need any money for the second one until I was well into it. You can accomplish a fair amount without money, though money may become a factor as your vision grows, changes and develops.

If you do need money, begin by writing a list of 10 possible ways to get it. You may be surprised at your own genius if you give it enough thought. Go down the list and rate each idea from 1 to 10—1 being the most feasible and 10 being your last resort. Then get out there and start the wheels rolling.

It's far easier to get people to underwrite a project that has seen some small successes than a project that is still a pipe dream. Decide what you want to accomplish with the funds you are seeking and communicate that in a clear way to potential supporters.

Time

Your most precious resource is time. Most visions take a lot of time to develop and implement, and you must find the time necessary to achieve yours. To accomplish this, you will have to cut out some activities and live life a little differently.

For example, if I attend a wedding, I don't attend the reception because it would take up half a day that needs to be spent elsewhere. It is too time-consuming for me. My church is full of young people, so there is never a shortage of receptions to attend. If I were to go to each, I would do nothing else and end up a professional glutton! Besides, you usually don't get a chance to talk to the bride and groom at the reception anyway.

I urge you to lead a balanced life in every possible way. Have fun and allow yourself to be renewed; however, be careful not to take your down time to the extreme. We often indulge in too many leisure activities, especially earlier in life when we have fewer responsibilities. These activities can become a hindrance to your vision, so balance is the key.

Obviously, you have as much time as anybody else does. When you get up every morning, you have the same 24 hours that a president, a prime minister and the pope have. Each of us has the same amount of time; it's what you do with that time that matters. If you wish to accomplish great things for God, you must be disciplined with your time. Nonbelievers aren't working for the eternal state of souls, yet they make incredible sacrifices to achieve their goals. Some of them get up at 4:00 A.M. and go to bed at midnight day after day, year after year, to accomplish their temporal goals. Imagine what would happen if we approached our God-given visions with similar tenacity! You don't need to turn into a workaholic; simply become deliberate, thoughtful and intentional about the use of your time.

The Beginning

As with most things in life, taking the first step towards fulfilling your vision is always the hardest. Visions do not arrive from heaven in a hand basket. If you received a vision for a Soul Survivor conference, 20,000 people wouldn't just drop in at the festival site a week later. Most organizations boast about their small beginnings, because they grew a little bit at a time.

A few years ago a theological student in my church felt frustrated at his lack of opportunity for evangelism. He only met Christians at the college he attended and was getting sick of it. He continually prayed, *What can I do? What can I do?* Then God began to form a vision within him.

This happened in the days before drugs made AIDS more manageable. At that time, many more people were dying from this disease and AIDS hospices were being built so that people could live out the final days of their lives as comfortably as possible.

So the Lord put a vision in this young man's heart. In order to evangelize people who were sick and dying, why not go to those hospices? The vision stirred in him and he prayed about it, then God confirmed it. It stirred many times after that, and God confirmed it in various ways. The intensity of the vision grew, until finally one day he got so frustrated that he finally thought, *I've got to do something.*

He did not run back to church to receive another prophecy, to attend an all-night prayer vigil or to get zapped by God one more time. There was no longer a need for that. At this point, he just got out the phone book, opened it to the "AIDS Hospices" section, picked up the phone and dialed. **To begin is the key!**

He called many hospices, saying, "I'd like to come out and minister, love, care and show compassion for the people there." The first 25 hospices replied, "Well, if you want to do that, you have to go through three years of training and possess a degree."

He thanked them and moved along to the next number until he finally heard, "We'd love to have you. Here is our address; come up and see us."

When he arrived, the director met him, liked him and told him to stop by whenever he wished. Thus began his regular visits to the hospice. **To follow through is the next key step.** The first time he entered the hospice the nurses strapped him into a space suit, complete with gloves, hood and mask. As he tried to strike up conversations with the hurting people there, they showed little interest in talking to an astronaut. He began to feel that Jesus would have put His hands on these people. So one day, with the hospital's permission, he took off the suit and sat by their beds, holding their hands and talking to them. He cracked jokes, laughed at their jokes, earned their trust and just loved them. Up to this point, he hadn't even mentioned the name of Jesus; he simply demonstrated His love.

Slowly, one by one, the patients began to open up and talk about life, death and spirituality, and he began leading people to Jesus. I cannot recall the number of patients we baptized on their deathbeds in that place.

It was great, but you know what? Nobody would go with him. Nobody would participate. He had to do it all by himself—*until it was a success*. Then everybody wanted to go with him. That's how it is in the Church; nothing succeeds like success. Somebody has to go first and take the first step. Little successes have a way of leading to other things as you get going. Now that same guy is planting a church in San Francisco that ministers to the gay community.

Some time later, a guy who had recently become a Christian had an urge to do something similar. He had heard the stories about the success at the AIDS hospice so he asked around, found out the name of the hospice and phoned them. They said that they would love to have him, so he went and began to meet regularly with the patients there.

One day he noticed that the patients did not have fruit to eat. So one day he went to the market and arrived at the hospice with some fruit. With hospital permission, he handed out the fruit. As he did this, one of the patients approached him (thinking he was a priest) and said, "Well, when are you going to do a service for us?"

He later told me what had happened. I encouraged him, and as his pastor, gave him the go-ahead. Only having been a Christian for six months, he asked me what he should do in the way of a service. I told him to play worship CDs on a portable CD player and to read some Scripture, not wanting to discourage him with complicated details.

After a couple of these services he returned to me and said, "Now they want me to serve Communion!"

As our church is Vineyard, I told him, "Get some bread, break it, pour the grape juice, say these things, hand it out and you can have Communion."

The patients were thrilled with Communion and asked him to preach. When he told me the news, I replied, "Okay, let's sit down and have a little talk."

We never sent someone to bail him out; we let God lead him. One thing led to another, and before long he was leading a regular service with Communion, a sermon and even a congregation. He took the first step—he went. Then things started to happen.

Anything worth doing is worth starting now and fixing later. Don't wait until you think you have every question answered and all the details worked out to perfection. Notice I said *think*. If you formulate your plans before you get involved, you will find that they do not match up to the realities, and the plan will go out the window. Get there, start the process, be involved and you'll find out what's really needed. Then you can come up with a plan and fix problems along the way.

As I said earlier, I started my church by accident. I met a married couple who agreed with me that you could actually worship with guitars—at that time, most churches did not use guitars. I wanted a service where the Holy Spirit could really move, and this couple sought the same thing. I said, "Let's have a prayer meeting at your house," and they agreed. They thought it would just be the

three of us. For a couple of weeks it was, but then it grew. Three months later, 90 people came to their house every week.

It starts with one person, who takes the first step, to fulfill one God-given vision. If you want to start a homeless shelter, start by finding out where the homeless are right now in your community; then simply go there and be with them. To start churches in bars, get a group who share your vision, find a bar that will rent you a spot and open the first service. The first step is yours to take.

Basic Strategy

Get started and work on your strategy as you go. These points are in a deliberate order. Unless you are really experienced in whatever your vision is, you need to be out there before you can plan the strategy. Of course, strategy does not mean that every last detail is laid down. Every vision develops in stages.

The initial stage is followed by several stages of growth, each one leading to the next. All you need to do is plan for the next stage. Now is not the time to figure out what you are going to do when your vision goes international and reaches every continent. Don't worry about that; worry about how you are going to get to the next neighborhood. Take it one stage at a time.

Momentum

Create small successes. As you see people's lives change and things come together, celebrate with your team. If you create a sense of momentum, your team's faith in what can happen will increase. A few small successes in hand will enable you to build from there.

Your Relationship with God

Guard yourself against crashing and burning. Take care of your relationship with God, your integrity and your emotional and physical health. The most common vision killer is failing to begin; the next most common is a weary visionary—a great vision caster who has lost heart. If you don't take care of yourself, you will set yourself up for discouragement and moral failure.

You don't have to do everything in a day. Don't listen to yourself when you think, *I have to do it all in the first six months!* In fact, there is very little you can do in six months. But you can accomplish a huge amount in five years—ironically, almost always more than you think.

Question: How do you achieve a balance between vision and ambition?

Steve Nicholson: Godly vision centers on accomplishing something for God and His people; ambition centers on my position in that vision. It is possible, however, to have an ambition to be fully used by God in the vision He has given you. I would rather work with someone who has a lot of mixed ambitions—godly and personal—and let experience beat out the latter than with an individual deprived of both. In all honesty, it is difficult for anyone to completely avoid mixed ambitions. How many of us came to Christ with entirely unselfish motives? Yet He didn't deny us entry into His kingdom or throw us out the door. Start with what you have. I often hear older pastors criticize some leaders who are in their early 20s: "He's a little bit arrogant don't you think?" I reply, "So? I was arrogant. We were all arrogant at that age." The best cure is involvement: Let them get out into the battle. God will take care of their arrogance through experience. Making mistakes and discovering limitations does wonders for an overworking ego! The worst possibility is to be arrogant while sitting on the sidelines—for that there is no cure. Ambition is a tame beast compared to a sideline critic who never does anything. That's why ambition doesn't worry me so much.

Q: Are most visions preceded by some kind of wilderness experience in which a leader feels isolated, depressed or removed from society?

SN: The Bible recounts many wilderness experiences during which a vision is realized. But there are also many times when the wilderness experience comes later, in the midst of an unfolding vision. I didn't really hit the wilderness in my life until halfway through the realization of my vision. Regardless of when the wilderness experience comes, I can guarantee you will experience the dry, monotonous, seemingly endless desert at some point. As hopeless as the situation may feel at the time, you will get through the wilderness in the same way the rest of us have: by yelling, screaming, crying out to God and waiting on Him, and somehow—by His grace—you'll crawl across the line.

Q: What's your perspective on competition between churches or ministries? How do you deal with other groups that might feel competition with your group?

SN: Competition: You start something and others feel that you are threatening their territory. This is one of my pet peeves, so forgive my lengthiness. Unfortunately, some Christians think that we are competing with each other. If you view your brother as your enemy, you are in a truly sad state. Your competition is not the church across town, but television, bars, the Internet, drugs and the devil! That should be enough competition for you.

We are not in competition. Just as with the wall that Nehemiah and the Israelites built, we all have to work on different sections, doing different tasks; but we all have the same goal: to get the thing built! We must learn how to be Kingdom minded. You shouldn't be asking yourself how someone else's ministry is going to affect you and your ministry. That is a sign of insecurity and Christian immaturity, and that kills the Church.

I have seen crazy things. Imagine a church nestled in a corner of a city of 1 million people. Imagine the audacity to feel threatened by another church moving into the other side of the city. We need a hundred churches in that city! Let's grow up and get over ourselves. Every leader in the history of the Church who has started something new and significant has faced opposition because people have felt threatened by the new. Read the journals of John Wesley. Read about all the trouble he got into with people who were afraid that their parishioners would listen to Wesley with his new style of doing things.

If God has called you to a vision and if there are thousands and thousands to be reached but only one being threatened, move forward. Be gracious and stay in a relationship with him or her, but by all means, don't let him or her stop you.

We are all on the receiving end for a time. If you start your new group, maybe next year someone will decide that your area is big enough for two groups. If you are so insecure that you are afraid of losing all your people to a better group, maybe you should lose all your people. If they really are better, close down and join them!

If God is behind your vision, nothing can threaten it—not even a new, flashier group. Of course, if your vision is just a human thing, then someone else's supernatural vision might just put you out of business. That's okay! Let it happen. The Church does not suffer from a surplus but from a lack of effective churches, groups, leaders and outreaches.

Q: If a husband and wife have different ideas in terms of vision, how do they serve one common vision, or should they do that?

SN: First, it is very important for a married couple to be in agreement about a significant vision. It is nearly impossible to pursue a vision that your spouse does not agree with. That does not mean that your spouse has to have the same gifts or the same role as you in fulfilling the vision. But your spouse must agree that it is from God and be prepared to participate on whatever level is necessary.

For example, my wife and I are very different. She does not particularly enjoy public speaking. She is more of a behind-the-scenes person. Her particular gifts make her the world's best assistant and intercessor. I couldn't carry out my vision without her. At big events, I love jumping down in the ministry pit and praying for anybody I can get my hands on. She, on the other hand, would much rather sit in the back, interceding for the whole thing or praying for specific people she sees at a distance.

We have different personalities, gifts and roles, but we are both totally convinced that what we are doing is God's will. We discuss which trips I should go on, and most of the time, she thinks that I should go even when I do not want to. I often have hesitations about all this and she will push me forward to go. We are unified in what we do, even though we participate on different levels.

Inevitably, your spouse will be deeply impacted by any vision you have—God-given or not. Every vision has a price tag, and your spouse will end up paying the bill along with you.

If you aren't married, but already have vision burning within you, do not even begin the process of romancing someone unless they are willing to participate in that vision. Do not even think of marrying someone who isn't wholeheartedly committed to seeing God's will accomplished in your life. That is not the road to happiness. Once you fall in love with a person like that, it's already too late; don't pursue someone unless you know that you are spiritually compatible with that person.

I started my church before I got married. When I first met my wife, she didn't feel an independent call to church planting. But as the years passed, she came to support the vision God had given me and was prepared to walk the road beside me wherever God led us. By the time we married, she did feel called to what I was doing, and our call has worked out well.

Your spouse does not necessarily need to hear the call you hear, but he or she must be prepared to be a part of it. He or she must feel drawn into it, not forced, because his or her consent has to be genuine so that the commitment can endure what may be many years full of ups and downs. Your spouse has to be willing to raise your children in the situations in which you will find yourselves. I cannot stress enough how important it is to discuss and be realistic about these types of things early on in a romantic relationship.

If God stirs something in your heart that creates a disagreement in your marriage, don't pursue that vision until you and your spouse are in agreement. God sometimes organizes the timing of visions in this way. Sometimes a person receives a vision, but his or her spouse says, "I don't think so yet." Trust God as you wait for His timing. Trust that God can speak to your spouse as He has spoken to you. The God who spoke to Balaam through a donkey and brought water out of rocks can certainly confirm a vision to a spouse who is willing to conform to His will.

Note

1. Vince Lombardi, quoted at *Quote World*. http://www.quoteworld.org/author.php?thetext=Vincent%20Thomas%20&page=2 (accessed March 31, 2004).

Chapter Six

TOP 10 MOST COMMON MISTAKES LEADERS MAKE

One of my church planters came to me as we were getting ready to send him out. It was a pretty scary moment for him, as he was leaving the comforts of home to start something new. "I'm just so afraid of making mistakes," he said.

I replied, "Stop worrying about it—you will."

Everyone makes mistakes. In fact, my biggest fear is that you don't make any mistakes because that usually means you've made the worst mistake of all—sitting at home twiddling your thumbs. I want you to get out in the game and participate, which inevitably leads to the occasional error. However, over the years I have found some common mistakes that can eventually become real difficulties if not caught early on.

I have witnessed all of these mistakes while working with young leaders over the years. I hope this outline will help you avoid these common pitfalls; then you can then go out and make some new mistakes of your own.

You will make mistakes, but I am confident that you won't make nearly as many as I have, and I'm still standing. God built His Church and His plan will not be thwarted; so rest assured that what is from God will survive. All that is required of you is that you learn from every mistake that you make.

Not Taking Risks

The first big mistake young leaders make is neglecting to embrace risk. You must take the first step without waiting for things to be fully developed and organized. Try new things, remembering that failure shouldn't keep you from trying again. You can fail and recover, especially when you are young. If the risk you take ends up a dead end, chalk it up to experience and add that idea to your list of things to avoid in the future.

Among church planters there is a stigma about 20-somethings as opposed to individuals in their late 30s to mid-40s with more life experience. Each age group has its advantages but people trust middle-aged pastors more readily thinking that gray hair signifies knowledge. (I know better! I have met some gray-haired people who were more foolish than they were at age 20.) On the other hand, older people have pressures, obligations and families. They need to keep the money coming in and guard the stability in their life, so they tend to do church planting by the book. The disadvantage, of course, is that these older guys tend to miss out on the unexpected things that actually help make a church work because they're afraid to experiment.

For example, I was having a hard time getting a church going in Chicago. When God finally moved me out of leadership there, we got a new pastor who was younger than me. He experimented more. One thing he stumbled across was the idea of weekends away. He would take the people of this small church into the country on weekends. The church members invited their non-Christian friends and relatives who had never been out to the country. While in the country, they orchestrated times where they preached the gospel and a few people shared what Jesus had done in their lives. On every trip, about half the non-Christians who went returned knowing Jesus. Who would have thought you could reach city people by taking them to the

country? Churches like that grow and multiply because young leaders often stumble across great ideas.

Being young is great—you have plenty of time to experiment, fail and try again. If you are older, be as creative as you can so as not to get stuck in a rut. If you can, ally yourself with some really creative young people and listen to their ideas. This exchange might make it work.

Keep your eyes open for the unexpected, because the fulfillment of a vision is not our plan. In the end it's God's plan, so make sure you're willing to take risks.

Controlling Behavior

Leaders get frustrated with their people. Workers turn up late, aren't committed, won't volunteer, and frequently get their lives into messes. As leaders get exasperated, they use other means to get people to clean up their behavior. They create social pressures or certain rules, telling the individuals to submit to their pastors. They ask them to make more commitments. They may even employ the tried and true guilt routine.

Trying to control others' behavior from the outside in never works. You may acquire the temporary compliance of a few (who grit their teeth and build up anger and resentment against you), but your control won't move or change anyone's heart. If you as a leader need to remind people to follow you, take a good, long look in the mirror. Reevaluate your reasons and motivations. Question your goals; compliance or behavioral changes shouldn't be one of them. Read the New Testament and you'll find that the Pharisees were looking to control.

The Pharisees were zealous for righteousness and holiness. They defended the Scriptures but forgot that the work of God begins on the inside and works itself out. The reason they had so many disagreements with Jesus was because they had their theology backward. Jesus wanted to win hearts and minds, not simply change the way people acted. Our aim should be the same.

I feel sorry for Christian leaders who fall into this trap. To use an Old Testament metaphor, they are selling their birthright for a mess of porridge. They settle for temporary obedience followed by future blowups and conflicts, instead of the bigger victory won by encouraging people's hearts and minds. People should not feel compelled to act in a particular way because leaders are looking over their shoulders, but because Christ has transformed their lives.

Sixteen years ago I was on my first trip to the United Kingdom. In the plane I was arguing about something with a friend. I was still caught in this behavior problem, and I pushed him on one point. He suddenly turned to me and said, "You're winning this argument but losing my heart."

It was as if the bottom fell out of me. Have you ever had your eyes opened to see that you were sinning without knowing it? My heart sunk down into the Atlantic Ocean. I saw the wrong and changed immediately. Bless God that I changed because we are still working together.

In the end, people you lead will eventually follow their own beliefs about themselves and God. If leaders have trouble with their motivations for ministry, the problem is probably their messy relationship with God. If your workers are healthy and have experienced the glory of God through the Holy Spirit, you won't have to push them into ministry.

Taking On Unnecessary Responsibility

Let's get something straight: As a leader, you're not responsible for widespread happiness or welfare. You don't need to treat everybody like children by catering to their every need. A young man once phoned me to ask if I could find him an apartment. I said I wouldn't. He protested on the grounds that

I'm a pastor. My answer was, "So what? You're 25 years old and an adult. Look in the paper and find an apartment on your own like everybody else." You are not responsible for every problem, need or action people may take. Let them be stupid when they want to be. Your job is to teach from the Word of God, to be an example and to do that which you have agreed to do within the bounds of your ministry.

Bearing unnecessary burdens will only lead to rapid burnout. Do your part, let Jesus do His, and understand the difference. Your job is to share the good news of what Jesus has done in your life, that He is alive and that He loves people. It is not your job to convert people—that task belongs to the Holy Spirit. Understand whose part is whose, and don't step beyond your realm of control.

Take care that you do not go too far in trying to protect people from their own mistakes, particularly if your role is a pastoral one. If they're going to violate the moral laws of the Bible, they must suffer the consequences. Speak strongly, and explain how he or she will violate biblical authority.

Still, there may be situations when the issue isn't black and white. For example, a new Christian gets a job that takes him or her too far away from the fellowship, and you are

not sure that he or she will be all right. That is a matter of wisdom, in which case you have to approach the individual with tact. Talk through the problems and the repercussions the decision may have, but leave the decision up to the person.

Allow people to make their own decisions and leave room for them to do things you may consider a mistake. If they ask you for advice, give it to them. However, beware of crossing over into manipulation, which can easily become spiritual abuse.

A part of each of us feels the need to protect people from their mistakes, but does God protect you from all of yours? He gives you plenty of latitude to go out and learn the hard way; so let your people learn some things the hard way as well. As mentioned earlier, often there's no substitute for a lesson learned in the fire of difficulty.

Not Developing Your Relationship with God

Mother Teresa's work in India should have been a high-burnout ministry. She ministered to the poorest of the poor, picked those who were in the process of dying, sat with them and loved them until they were gone; then she did it all over again. She and her staff should have burned out early on, but they didn't. Why? Because she insisted that all who worked with her spend an hour every day with Jesus before doing anything else. She was adamant that they feed themselves spiritually before going out into the world to feed the poor. She required that they first take care of their own relationship with God.

As a leader, don't let stress destroy your relationship with God. Your role as a leader ranks far below your role as a child of God. There must be a place where you cease to be in charge and allow your heavenly Father to take charge of your life.

I tell people that the first item on my prayer agenda is to be the best follower of

Christ I can be. Then I focus on the other parts of my life, including my ministry and vision. If you don't take care of your relationship with God, you won't have enough in you to make it to the end.

SETTLING FOR LESS

Here is the situation:

> You need something done.
> There is a warm body nearby.
> You ask him or her to do the task
>   that needs to be done.

What is the result? Often the leader finds out too late that the person has a problem with commitment, character or gifting. The leader felt such an urgency to see the task fulfilled that he or she put any warm body in there to fill the gap, and then regretted it.

I see this scenario played out often among church planters: The first thing they want is a worship leader, so they grab the first singer/guitarist they can find. Afterward, they find that the guy has trouble showing up on time, isn't responsive to the pastor, sings out of tune or argues with those with whom he works. Unfortunately, by the time this stuff fleshes out, the guy has made a lot of friends and problems start, all because the church planter jumped a little too quickly. I hear this lament often: "We promised this guy he's going to be our next full-time worship pastor, but he can't even function at this level. We've found someone else we want to hire! What are we going to do?" All you can do is fire the first guy, but it will be painful for him and his friends. What's the moral of this story? Wait until you've found the right person.

When the prophet Samuel went to anoint the next king of Israel at the house of Jesse, Jessie's sons were brought out and displayed before Samuel (see 1 Samuel 16:1-13). God didn't instruct the old prophet to choose the best looking, the tallest, the most handsome or the most charismatic of the bunch. As a

matter of fact, God chose the son that Jesse didn't even think to ask to attend the party that day. He chose the little shepherd out in the field—the youngest of them all. Samuel waited until God pointed him to the right person. It wasn't just a matter of grabbing the most popular guy and putting a crown on his head. David was out there, but Samuel had to look around, be patient and listen to God's promptings.

My point is that you must wait until God says, "Rise and anoint him; he is the one" (1 Samuel 16:12). This may mean holding back on some part of the development of your ministry, but delay is much better than having the wrong person. Learn how to humbly ask the Father's permission. Carefully consider your criteria before you start to put people into long-term positions. Make sure you are clear about job descriptions, commitment and character, and that you have tested their gifting. These areas are crucial when searching for future leadership candidates.

Concentrating on Problems

I once discovered that some of our church plants reached about 50 people and then hit a plateau. When I investigated, I found out that when the churches reached 50 people, the members of the church no longer felt the need for more people. Typically, people have active social circles no larger than 50, and as a result, whenever a church reached that number, people were happy.

The pastor of one church in particular found himself fully occupied every day of the week, coping with the needs of his 48 church members, and keeping up with the active church calendar. Thus, he wasn't able to reach people outside the church. I told him that if he wanted the church to grow beyond 50 people, he would have to cut his schedule in half and force himself to take care of his present load in half as much time. Obviously, he would need to train up young leaders to help him accomplish the task. Next, he would need to take the remaining half of his time to reach another 50 people. He would need to get out there and recruit people as if he were beginning with an entirely new church. The church began to grow again, partly because they became proactive in their outreach and ceased to focus only on the inner needs and problems of the church.

There is always more than one way to solve a problem, but you have to think creatively. Too often we say we are stuck with a problem and have to stop, when really there are 10 more ways to reach a resolution. Learn how to sit down and think up those 10 different ways, rather than letting your progress slow down. If you can't go over the mountain, go around it. If you can't go around the mountain, tunnel through it; and if that fails, tear the darn thing down! There is always more than one way to deal with a mountain, and there are always many ways to solve a problem.

Don't let the little problems cloud your vision and goals by allowing the problems to become the focus of your talks, planning and time. Prioritize your problems. At staff meetings with the church team, we always put our main priorities and objectives at the top of the agenda and little problems that need solving at the bottom. Whatever is at the top of the agenda is given the most time, and whatever is at the bottom gets hurried. Put the problems at the bottom of your agenda so that you spend less time on them.

Not Addressing Your Own Weaknesses

You need accountability, but it doesn't come unless you tell the truth to the people to whom you're accountable. Learn how true accountability works so that you can win your battles before they become struggles.

The biggest strength God gives us in dealing with our weaknesses is each other. If we don't work side by side in honesty, confessing our sins to one another, using our various gifts to complete one another and move forward, our weaknesses will overwhelm us.

Part of teamwork is learning to listen to those who think differently from you. This is important when you understand a strange dichotomy: For every gift or strength you possess, you will also possess a corresponding weakness. If you have a gift of prophecy,

you likely have a passion for justice, see things about people and their lives that others don't, and may be more sensitive to the move of the Spirit. One of your great weaknesses may be that you have no sense of how to build things or lead groups. If you're a pastor, you probably organize, nurture and build community very easily, but you may be weak when it comes to issues of direct confrontation and intuition.

The pastors and the prophets, as well as many other groups in the Church, have difficulty understanding each other. Sometimes it seems as if God enjoys putting terribly mismatched individuals on the same team. But the Lord pairs opposites together so that one can cover the weaknesses of the other. This is truly what Paul meant when he wrote about being the Body of Christ.

Not Admitting Mistakes

We have already discussed the importance of admitting when you are wrong. Still, the point is worth repeating. Take responsibility for your mistakes, because in the end, it is the best and most godly way of handling a situation where you've slipped up.

Often when you have conflicts with people, you'll find that 10 percent of the fault is yours and the other 90 percent falls on the other person's shoulders. Don't waste your time trying to argue with him or her about what he or she has done wrong. Admit your 10 percent and let the rest go. In the long run, that attitude can help diffuse even the most tense situations.

Leading Without a Team

Trying to fulfill a vision without a team is a huge mistake. As we discussed earlier, nothing is impossible for the man or woman who does not have to do it alone.

Thinking Too Small

Think big dreams, ask the Lord what He's calling you to achieve for Him and allow Him to stretch your vision.

Q & A

Question: Do you have to be married to be a pastor or to be in leadership?

Steve Nicholson: No. I started two churches before I married. Jesus wasn't married. Neither Paul nor Samuel were married.

Q: My chaplain recently left—I want to know how to deal with the transition.

SN: Dealing with the transition that comes with a new leader is often difficult. First, begin fervently praying that God will send the right person to fill the position. When the new person comes, it's incredibly important that you get to know that person, understanding that he will be quite different from the previous leader. Very seldom is the next person similar to the previous one, so be prepared for some changes—even drastic ones—and take them as God's will. Try to learn from the differences and work with the situation as it is. Become as much of a servant to your new leader as you can. He must earn your trust, and you will have to do likewise, by serving together and communicating with one another.

Q: How do you inspire a team of volunteers with full-time jobs and little time?

SN: First, as the leader, make sure that your events are as organized as possible. If people show up to work and no one knows what's going on, they will become discouraged quickly.

The second way to motivate and inspire a crew is to communicate their potential to them. Help them see that in four hours on a Saturday morning they can achieve something of great value. They will feel significant if they know that they have a definite role in fulfilling a vision. They are there because they want to do something for God—more than just sitting there and making money. Your job is to show them how to do it realistically.

Finally, understand their situation in life. If they're single, they're usually full of energy and can stay up late and do more for you. However, if they have young kids, there's no way they can do that. That does not mean they are less committed to Jesus. They have not lost their first love. They are simply at a different stage in life. You must then adjust the amount of time and energy they contribute, so they will not feel overwhelmed or get burned out. Do your best to communicate that they are just as significant and meaningful to the group.

Q: When trying to address your own weaknesses and seek accountability, to whom should you go? Should it be an older mentor or peer?

SN: It doesn't matter what the age, as long as the individual will not let you off the hook too easily. You want him or her to ask you the nasty questions—the questions none of us want to hear, much less answer. You want someone who will not let you get off with half a confession. When confessing sin, most people tell half the facts because they are too ashamed to tell everything.

A few years ago, I traveled over the summer and when I returned one of the guys from my church came to see me. I could tell he wasn't doing well. Our conversation went something like this:

"So, how was your summer?"

"Well, I've had a really bad summer."

"Oh really? What was bad about it?"

"Well, I met this girl, and—you know—we had troubles in our relationship."

"What kind of troubles did you have in your relationship?"

"Well, you know . . . We kind of had trouble managing the physical side of our relationship."

"Oh really? Well, what did you do?"

"Well . . . it wasn't that bad. It was just kind of difficult."

"Oh. Umm. . . did you have sex with her?"

"No. Not exactly."

"Well what exactly did you do? Did you take her clothes off?"

"Well, yeah."

"Did she take your clothes off?"

"Well yeah, once."

It continued like that and I just continued to ask more and more explicit questions. In the end we uncovered that he had been having sex with her all summer long and he felt guilty. He then said, "I wanted you to ask me all those questions. I wanted you to catch me. I just couldn't bring myself to come out and say it." He came to me because he knew that I would not let him off with a half confession. I would not stop at "We just had some physical problems."

When someone has cancer, you can't stick an adhesive bandage on it. If you had cancer, you wouldn't want a mealymouthed surgeon who simply says, "Okay, let's just take out a little of this—it's not that bad." You would want someone who understands that you have to get every last bit out. If somebody is trying to confess a weakness—or a cancer in his or her life—make him or her go right down to the ugly, nasty bottom so that he or she can really deal with God. Find a friend who will play straight with you. He or she will be your best friend in the world.

Q: No matter what we do, we always start every event 15 minutes late. How can we get our service started on time?

SN: Starting late is an infamous problem in the Church. I spent about 15 years wrestling with this problem. I tried harassing, preaching and explaining the need for punctuality. We tried changing the start time to 15 minutes later, but of course everyone just came 15 minutes later than the new time. There is only one solution: just start on time. If only two people are there, start anyway. Make whatever you open with so good that people who aren't there on time miss out. If you keep all the good stuff till the end, when the most people are there, you reward their tardiness.

You must be a behavioral scientist about such things; it's all about rewards and punishments. If the event is early in the morning, offering coffee or food beforehand helps people get there on time. Alternatively, meet at a venue that doesn't contain enough seats so that people must stand in line for them. This will also encourage punctuality.

Q: We want to start cell groups, but some are for it and some against the change. How can we encourage unity on this subject?

SN: Often, when you try to change your group, whether in culture or in structure, your people will fall into different groups. Some will be for the new move, some will follow without eagerness, and some will be totally against it. Every group divides in this way when introduced to change. You can help matters by explaining the reasons behind the change and giving them time to process the information. Let the middle camp sell it to those who are slow to accept it. Try to keep the radicals from selling too much because they tend to alienate the traditionalists. Use those in the middle to win others over.

Let things evolve slowly. Tell reluctant people that they can keep doing their thing in their corner for a while if they like, while the rest of you work on the new project. If you tell people that the change is a six-month experiment with a reevaluation at the end, they will accept it more easily. Then at the end of the designated time, you can evaluate and see whether you want to keep going or not. Strangely enough, the traditionalists will usually grump and complain all the way up to the next change. Then they become traditional about the previous change you made. Traditionalists are great at maintaining things, so use that skill if you can. Put them in positions where maintaining the status quo is appropriate.

Chapter Seven

HOW TO MULTIPLY LEADERS

DISCOVER THE LIMITING FACTOR

The number one factor limiting the effectiveness of our churches and ministries is a lack of dynamic leadership. The impact leadership has on an organization—positive or negative—is staggering. The quality of leadership determines church attendance, the effectiveness of ministries and the long-term growth of the organization.

At a gathering of North American pastors and leaders that I once attended, we discussed the ominous state of failing leadership. I asked the group if they knew of any cases that didn't follow the trend; in other words, which churches were growing and reaching young people? They named a few places, and we tried to discover what it was that made these ministries unique. After much discussion, we found a distinct pattern: Every instance of thriving, growing ministry had dynamic leadership and a system for multiplying that leadership.

Most people will admit that they always want more leaders. I rarely run into a church leader who would tell a prospective volunteer, "No, thank you. I feel I have enough leaders right now." I have often been asked how I always seem to have so many leaders. Perhaps you also wonder why Mike Pilavachi always has so many leaders within Soul Survivor.

You can help develop this pattern of dynamic, multiplication of leadership in your own unique context. Believe it or not, you can actually have more control over the number of leaders you have. To find out how, let's look at three things you don't want to do. The following are the attitudes and actions that will hinder you from having a dynamic, energetic team of leaders.

1. Insecurity and Control

The number one hindrance to multiplying leadership is personal insecurity. To multiply leaders, you have to let people follow somebody else; you must let leaders other than yourself lead and let people follow them. You even have to let people develop loyalty to them. This demands a certain amount of letting go. You must willingly accept the uncertainties of leading through other leaders, which requires trusting them to develop to their full potential—and allowing them to make mistakes.

This principle is played out for us in 1 Samuel 18. Before David was king, he was a loyal subordinate who fought battles for Saul. He would never do anything to harm the king. However, when people started showing loyalty for David and began to follow him, Saul's insecurity in his own leadership drove him mad. He simply could not accept it. In the end, this mix of jealousy and insecurity caused Saul to lose everything.

Insecure church leaders recruit leaders who lead for a little while, become discouraged and demoralized, and then leave. Then those same leaders recruit a new group, who in time do the same thing, and the pattern repeats itself. No leader stays for very long when the insecure leader of that church or ministry regularly trims the roles down to whatever he or she can directly control.

If you struggle with insecurity, it's time you clarify God's call in your heart. If God has put you in a place of leadership, you are the only one who can take it away! You must become totally secure in that knowledge.

Your primary concern should be your own actions, not the actions of others. At the end of the day, you are the only person who can screw things up. Sure, what others say about you can cause difficulties, but your biggest enemy is often the person looking at you in the mirror. Deal with your insecurities first and get over them once and for all. Since the beginning of time, every leader has received criticism and made a few mistakes. You have to build a tough skin, but keep a soft heart.

2. The Need to Be Needed

At our church of 700 people, we have a leadership team of approximately 120 people. I don't even know all the names of our leaders. Occasionally, I wonder what is actually going on in my church, what's happening under all these leaders. If I had restricted the leadership team to a specific number, I could sensibly lead it myself; but not only would we have fewer than 120 leaders, we would be lucky to have 120 people attending. If you want to multiply leaders, you must pay the price of losing some direct control and involvement. Unfortunately, many leaders are too insecure to release people into those roles.

Getting into ministry to fill a personal need to be needed is detrimental. It is one of the warning signs of an insecure leader and strains the multiplication of leaders. If you have been blessed with gracious and gifted leaders, they will do what you ask them to do with excellence. And suddenly you may not be needed as much, or at least you will feel that way.

If you begin to feel the pangs of unimportance, back up a little. Learn how to lead the leaders, as opposed to just leading the people. You must work through this with God, because the root of insecurity lies in a struggling relationship with God.

3. Visibility

You have too few leadership positions if the only positions you have available involve the use of microphones. In fact, you probably need approximately nine nonmicrophone positions for every one visible position in your ministry. Count the band members, teachers and moderators in your group. You now need nine times as many different kinds of leaders to have a healthy, growing, functioning ministry. If you are too focused on what is happening up front, you will have a great show without infrastructure, development or discipleship. When you emphasize the visible positions, you'll find yourself without enough spaces for your leaders. Leaders need jobs in which they can try things out.

Let's be honest, a good way to get people to come to church is to give them a job to do! On Sunday mornings in my church, we like to have a few jobs available for people who aren't even Christians yet. It is surprising how much more faithful they are than some of our Christians! They also feel pressure to show up, because if they don't, we won't eat. You see, we ask them to bring the food or make the coffee. After that of course, they are in the presence of God, hearing the gospel, around God's people and voila! It's usually not long before they come to God.

In fact, you may find that people will join the church community before coming to Christ. By witnessing the living Body of Christ in the context of our community life, they will come to faith. In giving them a job, you give them ownership and a chance to participate. To merely sit in the pew and listen is not enough. Do not focus on visible roles alone. Create more opportunities for people to get involved.

IDENTIFY LEADERS

Identifying potential leaders may be a difficult step in your quest to multiply leadership in your church or ministry. Which individuals will be the leaders of tomorrow? How can we begin to see them with clear eyes? There are two key principles to remember when seeking new leadership.

1. Look to the Heart

If you overlook character issues, you will get burned. Most leaders make the mistake of looking to the wrong people too quickly. Soon after, they learn the steep price for not

giving these individuals a second look. They discover that character is more critical than gifting. If you have to choose between a very gifted person with some character issues and a less gifted person with sterling character, you will learn to choose the latter every time. It's easier to teach a person necessary skills than it is to transform his or her character.

For example, we wanted to introduce a drummer into the worship band at church. We had several professional drummers in our fellowship, and we jumped at the chance to recruit these members for our band. But we soon realized that there was more to this situation than met the eye. Too many times the drummers couldn't make the necessary church meetings because of gigs, so we decided to train our own drummers. In any church there are always people who dream of being in a rock-and-roll band, so finding people who were willing to take paid drum lessons wasn't too difficult. As we selected these individuals, we were careful to make sure each was not only willing to pound away on Sunday mornings but was also a person of character.

Look first to the people you already have, because while they may not be as skilled as you would like, they have great character. Choose those with great character for ministry roles. They may need you to give them a little help, but chances are they will serve you well.

2. Look at the Source

Sometimes we can completely overlook our own source of leaders. I feel as though God assigns people to different leaders and churches, so I ask God which leaders are mine. One summer I walked around Soul Survivor wishing that some of the people were mine. God answered, "No, no, no—those are not yours!" That experience reminded me how important it is to know whom God has assigned to the ministry He has given me.

I recently officiated at a wedding. During the rehearsal I met a brother of the groom. The moment I laid eyes on him I thought, *Leader? Perhaps wandering in his faith a little bit.* I could immediately tell that he had been distant but that he had a real calling for leadership and needed to be with my group. I talked to him, asked questions and paid attention to him at the wedding rehearsal. Over the course of the wedding weekend, the life of the church completely blew him away. It was the first time he had been around Christians who were real and not just religious. We were full of joy, having fun and yet really serious about our faith. He had never seen anything like it, and it just blew his mind.

About a month later we invited him to come with us to do an outreach with another church. He came along, and we encouraged him to do things. We would be praying for people and we would ask him to come over and join us in prayer ministry. Of course, we hooked him in no time. Before long, he quit his job and moved to Chicago just to attend our church. Before he did, however, he visited another Vineyard church in another city with only 100 people that was desperate for leaders. He went there and thought, *I'm going to see if I get enthusiastic like I did at that church in Chicago.*

He tried to talk to the pastor, but the guy refused to talk to or pay any attention to him. So I got him. That often happens: The leaders are there in front of you, but you overlook the source. If you are a youth leader, your leaders are in your youth groups. They're right in front of you and all you have to do is let them lead.

At a Soul Survivor event one year, I got six or seven of my students from Chicago, ages 13 to 18, to do prophetic ministry for youth pastors. They did all the prayer and ministry on their own, and it was really powerful. A lot of youth leaders asked me how I got them to do it. I answered that I just *let* them do it. The students understand that I do not treat them as second-class ministers but as part of my army. In Chicago, they are part of the deal. On Sundays, I talk to them and ask them what is going on in their lives. I get them doing things so that I have less to do. During that ministry time at the Soul Survivor event, I just stood at the back and coached them a little. I acted like their safety net, so they felt secure. They knew that I was there in case things got sticky, but they did just about all the ministry. You would be surprised what students are able to do if you let them. If you are looking for leadership, start with your young people.

Young people live up to what you expect of them. If you expect them to do well, to be on fire for God and to do ministry, they will rise to the occasion. They're still teenagers, and the reality of hormones exists, so if you expect them to mess up and sin all the time, they will accommodate you.

With clear eyes you'll see your leaders. In Jesus' parable of the talents, the master gave one talent to one guy, three to another and five to a third guy. After a time, the men came back and the master asked them what they did with their talents. The master gave more talents to the men who made wise investments. The guy who buried his talent had it taken away (see Matthew 25:14-30).

God puts a certain number of leaders right under your nose. You must treat them well and see to it that they reach their full potential. Train them, develop them, and let them fly. Be secure enough to let them go, even if they make mistakes. Allow them to grow up and take on responsibilities.

As they develop and grow, they will yield more fruit for your ministry and for the Kingdom. Your leaders will multiply as long as you don't fill them with insecurity or stifle their development. If you hold onto them too tightly, like the servant who buried his talents, you will lose the leaders you have.

It's amazing how many times I come across young people who say, "We have this great vision! We want to do this ministry! We want to spread the gospel!" but their pastor or church board won't release them to fulfill that calling. I tell their church leaders that if they don't use them, I'll take them. If you don't utilize the leaders God gave you, He will give them to someone who will.

RECRUIT VOLUNTEERS

Recruiting for leadership is very different from recruiting volunteers for ministry. The latter is when you publish a notice in the church bulletin that reads something like this: "We desperately need someone to teach the class for the 13-year-old boys."

If you have tried that approach, you know full well that it doesn't really work. As a matter of fact, if you have tried something like that, you have sent out a whole host of negative messages.

- Every 13-year-old boy hears "I am at the bottom of the heap, and nobody wants to be with me."

- Every family hears "This church is not prepared to deal with 13-year-old boys."

- Potential volunteers hear "This must be the worst ministry in the church because nobody wants to do it."

This sort of approach has obvious flaws, but what are your alternatives?

Get rid of the leadership rotation in your groups. If you change leaders every week, you won't make any progress. You want someone who is called to youth work, has God's heart for youth and believes in them. You want someone who sees beyond the squirmy, loud-mouthed kid in the back row and sees the man or woman of God they will become. This sort of person can only be recruited.

Start by talking to God, rather than saying something in public. You could pray the following:

> *God, this is important. We've got to get to the heart of these kids. We need to get them on board so that by the time they're 17, they will lead the youth group. God, show me who is on your heart. Show me the person you're calling and send out a draft notice, God. Impress a burden on someone's heart that is so obviously from you, he or she can't escape it. Amen.*

Jesus said, "Ask the Lord of the harvest, therefore, to send out workers into his harvest field" (Matthew 9:38). You need to lift your future volunteers to God in prayer and ask Him to bring them to you. This may involve getting pretty passionate with God. Lying on the ground, yelling or screaming is acceptable here. It tends to work really well for me!

Ask God to show you the person who has the necessary qualities. Don't hesitate to be specific. In this example, I would ask for someone who

- Is slightly crazy

- Will build relationships with the students

- Laughs at 13-year-old humor

- Balances work and play (90 percent play, 10 percent work)

When you think you have found the right person, strike up a conversation with him or her: "Look, I need to talk to you. I have been asking God to show me the right person for one of the most important ministries in the church." Talk through the whole situation, including the bigger vision and this particular ministry's importance in that vision. Be sure to explain the level of commitment required—how many hours a week is required and so on. Then suggest that he or she pray and consider what God is asking of him or her. At that point, it's really between that person and the Lord.

REWARD LEADERS

All the leaders on your staff must be paid. However, that pay doesn't always have to be monetary as there are other kinds of currency. But some form of compensation for their work is necessary so that they'll want to continue their involvement. Would you want to serve if it entailed all work and no pay? Or would you end up feeling used by the church?

Pay them first with a relationship with you—the primary leader. When you recruit leaders for ministry, you have to understand that part of their pay is getting to spend time talking with you. If you want to lose all your leaders, starve them of your attention. To get more leaders, pay more attention to them!

Another form of pay is recognition. We all need to know that our work is appreciated. Don't hesitate to tell your leaders, "You did a great job there. I really appreciated the way you pushed through that difficult time with that kid and helped him get through. I noticed that you went beyond the call of duty." The Church is notorious for working people to the bone without so much as a "thank-you." Don't follow that trend. You will be surprised how little recognition costs and how tremendous the results are.

Between last Christmas and New Year's Day, I obtained the list of every single worker in our entire church with a list of the duties they performed. I had about 350 names on my list. Then I sat down and wrote out a short note to every single one, making mention of exactly what he or she had done during the previous year, how much it had meant to the church and the impact it had. Little gestures like that let people know that their service is appreciated and valued.

Pay can also include training and development opportunities. If you can build a reputation for offering people opportunities to grow and develop, you will have all the leaders you need. Take them to conferences, give them special goodies or share inside information. Help them see their position as an opportunity for personal growth and development, not as backbreaking labor to maintain the status quo.

By compensating your leaders, you will find that they will be more committed and that it will be easier to recruit new leaders. If you gain a reputation for using people up and throwing them away, the opposite will be true—it will only get harder and harder to recruit and maintain leaders.

Look at the Long-Term

The fourteenth church planter that we sent out from our church was in his late 20s and had only recently finished his theological training. I first noticed leadership potential in him when he was 15. I first met him at a conference. He was wearing a T-shirt that said "Party Naked," but I immediately thought, *Church planter*!

I saw his eyes, not the T-shirt. I saw fire in his heart, and I started to relate to this guy. I made the effort to encourage him. He went off to school and did various things, but through it all we stayed in touch. I encouraged him, paid attention to him, related to him and believed in him. Ten years later, I had a church planter who was sowing and reaping.

Don't neglect the long-term harvest. It took 10 long years with this young man, but he was well worth the effort.

Chapter Eight

MENTORING IN MINISTRY

INVESTING IN PEOPLE

At age 22 I read *The Master-Plan of Evangelism* by Robert Coleman. The title is misleading because it is not actually about evangelism but about discipleship and mentoring. It uncovers Jesus' chief strategy for turning the world upside-down. He worked hard to shape His 12 disciples because in the end the crowds disappeared; but the work of that core group had an immense lasting effect. After reading the book, I began to ponder the numbers.

Let's suppose you are a prolific evangelist, leading three people to the Lord every single day. That adds up to just over 1,000 people every year. If you evangelized that way for 20 years, without one person falling away from God, you would see approximately 20,000 people come to Christ.

Now let's suppose you're a better mentor than you are an evangelist, and you can disciple one individual a year. You invest in that person so that the following year he or she can lead and mentor one more disciple. The next year each of you trains another person, and so forth. You get the idea, but the results may surprise you. After 20 years you will have reached 1,048,576 people.

Looking at the numbers, which method is a better use of the time and resources God gave you? Either way, you're spending your life in ministry. The question is, Would you rather have just 20,000 people or more than 1 million to show for it? I decided to go for 1 million, since I'm not an evangelist of the three-people-a-day caliber anyway. But I can invest in one, two or even three individuals at a time, and thus have a larger impact over the course of my life. Since making that decision, I have always had a group of young men that I mentor and train. As a result, over the last 20 years our church has sent out more than 100 pastors and missionaries all over the world. And they're all doing the same thing in turn. My hope is that in the long run many of them will far surpass my ministry in scope and influence.

It's a lot more fun to watch someone you have trained succeed than to succeed yourself. Equipping those young people to do the prophetic ministry and to move in the Spirit that afternoon at the Soul Survivor event was much more fun than if I had done it myself. I came away from the afternoon excited—on a spiritual high. It was such a blast to watch their excitement build as they realized they could really do it. I loved it. I'm completely addicted to training and equipping young people to get out there and do likewise because it's a much better way of doing ministry.

Seeing the Pattern

From the beginning of the Bible to the end, we see that God works strategically. Elijah had Elisha, Moses worked with Joshua, and Naomi had Ruth. A fellow by the name of Joseph mentored Paul (Joseph eventually had his name changed to Barnabas, which means son of encouragement). Talk about a good mentor! It's interesting that later he and Paul had a falling out over John Mark. John Mark had messed up, and Paul was done with him. However, Barnabas wanted to give him a second chance. Barnabas ended up mentoring John Mark while Paul took another route with Silas (see Acts 15:36-40). But Barnabas was right about John Mark and the effect a good mentor can have even on a wayward disciple.

Start with a few key members of your youth group. Think and pray about them— God will show you who they are. It's amazing what young people can become with sustained investment, hope, attention and encouragement from a leader.

Value to Those Being Mentored

Personal attention from an experienced practitioner who can give advice like, "Try it this way," or "No, try it that way," helps young

leaders master their skills. Of course, this principle applies to any field of expertise. You always need someone to show you the ropes along the way, someone to help you make adjustments and encourage and guide you.

Mentoring is the key to developing leaders. You are not only passing on knowledge, you are imparting healthy attitudes, good character and a basic philosophy of ministry. But keep in mind, like children, those you mentor will pick up things you didn't necessarily intend for them to adopt. For example, those I have mentored tend to pray for people in a certain posture—one that looks strangely like mine. Those you train will pick up a lot more than just the explicit.

When I was attending university, we used to say, "Discipleship is caught more than taught." Hanging around people who are passionate and convicted is the surest way to become one of them because people tend to absorb the traits of those with whom they associate. When you find new believers, grab them and stick them with the most passionate crew. Soon, they will be as zealous as the rest of them.

The young leaders you mentor will also receive courage that wouldn't otherwise surface. At another Soul Survivor event one summer, I met a guy named James. During ministry time, I whispered in his ear, "Come on now, just walk on the water. Go out where you think you will sink. I'm here." I acted as the safety net that enabled him to step out, knowing that somebody was standing alongside him. Having an older person there to support a young leader through the rough spots can make a huge difference—it did for me.

As I became more involved in leadership, I got the chance to meet privately with a lot of leaders and speakers with platform ministries around the country. I became rather disillusioned as I discovered that, offstage, some of these leaders were real scumbags. No one could get along with them because they were terribly immature. There was a huge gap between what they said onstage and how they acted offstage. Obviously, not all of them were like this, but some who had been heroes shrank in my mind as I gained an inside perspective. As I struggled with the hypocrisy I saw, I became more and more cynical.

At that time, I had an opportunity to talk to John Wimber. I asked him how he dealt with the issue. He said, "Don't let the bad apples steal from you the joy of the good apples. I know there are some bad apples, but you also get the joy of serving alongside really great people—full of integrity—who are consistent in every context." He then began to rattle off names. His encouragement didn't change anything but my perspective, and that was all I needed to get through that rough spot.

That is what a mentor does. He or she talks you through something you run up against, and it can make all the difference in the world. I don't know what would have happened to me had John not taken the time to talk with me. Having someone who understands what is happening in your life and who believes in you enables you to press through some of the barriers and difficulties of leadership.

Value to the Mentor

One of my friends pastors a huge church. He once explained to me that if you ever lose sight of the faces, you lose your own sense of significance. You walk away from public speaking wondering whether it did anything for anyone. That's another reason why mentoring relationships are so vital—you witness change right before your eyes, which can fill you with a greater sense of purpose.

However, it is difficult to see the goalposts in ministry. When working with people, you can't really tally up the score at the end of the year and examine your success. You never reach the end of your to-do list in ministry, and as a result, a sense of progress may elude you. Just when you think you're doing well, one of the individuals you're mentoring will make a mistake, or a dispute will arise and you'll question your effectiveness as a leader. It is hard to hang on during those times, but if you stick with it, mentoring will prove to be one of the best places to see success.

Mentoring also forces you to develop as a person, because the teacher always learns more than his or her pupils. With passionate and committed young men and women barking at your heels and expecting you to invest in them, you're forced to keep learning.

Yet another value of mentoring is the multiplication of leadership we discussed earlier. The longer you mentor, the more you will have the burdens of ministry lifted as young leaders rise to carry your vision alongside you. Momentum builds because wherever you have leaders you will have people following. If you get the leaders, train them and invest in them, they will multiply your ministry tenfold.

Young people crave mentoring more than ever these days because so many aren't connecting with their families. Mom and Dad both work and probably never received the help they needed and never learned how to train their children in righteousness.

People will move heaven and Earth to be in a place where somebody will believe and invest in them. Strive to be such a person and you will never be short of potential leaders. Mentor them and you will benefit even more than they will.

Defining Mentorship

People often ask me for my mentoring program notes. Unfortunately, I cannot hand them over. It's not that the program is top secret—I simply don't have one. Mentoring is a *relationship*.

The Gospels tell us that Jesus called the disciples to be with Him and each relationship was unique. Likewise, I try to get to know the guys, and they get to know me. We spend time together: They travel with me; we work on projects together; I visit the events they put on; and we eat out and go to movies together. Just like friends, we take time to get accustomed to one another. Once you get into the relationship, the rest will come. I don't ever have to tell them, "I'll be your mentor." I just start. It may be a year before they realize what's really going on. Mentoring just happens as you constantly look for opportunities to get together.

Just as in Jesus' ministry, concentric circles will form. I focus most of my time and energy on the inner core: those who will be launching in a year or two. The next, slightly wider circle of leaders are about halfway through the process. The widest circle contains those who I'm thinking may get drawn in down the road. I work with all the individuals I'm mentoring; but just as Jesus had His three close friends among the 12, I focus the most on the inner core. I bring new young people into the outermost circle at the right times. As I do so, I ask God whether they need to be part of the process.

For those I mentor I am a listening ear, a brain to pick, a push in the right direction and a safety net. Sometimes I don't have to do anything—simply being there is enough. Other times I am their nemesis, challenging them and sticking them in situations that scare them but that help them grow.

About ten years ago, I knew this seminary student who had a phenomenal gift of prophecy, though he hadn't entered into it. I told him that I had to do a conference in another city

for a weekend and that I needed someone to come with me. He probably thought to himself, *Great, I'm going to carry Steve's bags.*

During the first meeting, about 10 minutes before the worship time ended, I leaned over to him and said, "Okay, I'm going to go up and preach for about 35 minutes. Then I'll call you up, and I want you to pick people out of the crowd and prophesy over them." He looked at me like he wanted to kill me, but he got up there, did a phenomenal job and hasn't stopped since.

Of course, you can't do that to just anybody. You must know whether this person has the gift and if he or she will be able to do the job. If you can see it, the key is to challenge him or her a little bit. If you provide too much warning, you provide excess thinking time and that can prevent someone from going with what's in his or her heart.

I learned this approach from John Wimber—firsthand. At the beginning of our relationship, when we had first started doing things together, he came to Chicago to do a large conference. He had decided he would teach me how to pray for the sick that day. So he got a sick person on stage and asked me to pray through each step while he commented for the people watching. I went for it, and God came and blessed us. After we finished with the first person and prayed for a couple more, he came over to me and said, "I don't know what to do next. Do you have any ideas?"

It took me 10 years to recognize that he was lying. I'm sure that he knew exactly what to do next, but he was working on me. At that time, I didn't know just how dangerous he could be, so when he asked me whether I had any ideas, I told him that I felt we ought to pray for people with a specific condition.

So he said, "Okay, that's a good idea. Go up to the microphone and announce that." Thousands of people had come to see John Wimber, so I went up there and said it. John then leaned over my shoulder and whispered, "I'm going back to the hotel now. You're in charge of the rest of the ministry time."

Before I could say anything he was gone, and my heart was pounding faster than normal. I wished he would stick around, but he knew exactly what he was doing. He wanted people who could do it themselves. Sometimes they just needed a little push.

Another time, we were halfway through a conference in Poland with a thousand pastors who had all made tremendous sacrifices to be there to hear from John Wimber. He turned to me during a worship time (as I was peacefully enjoying myself) and said, "You taught healing once in your church, didn't you?"

"Yes," I said.

"Good," he said. "Here are the notes. In 10 minutes get up and teach the class. You have until then to think of your stories."

That was it. I quickly learned to bring a briefcase full of teachings when traveling with him, as I never knew what to expect. The way he believed in me and constantly pushed me forward gave me confidence, and it was powerful. I wouldn't be in my position today if it weren't for all that John did with me.

Of course when John Wimber died, things continued on without a hiccup because there were people all over the world who he had trained and mentored. He was ruthless about it. He wasn't afraid to disappoint the crowds and force them to hear from an unknown young man from Chicago. He knew what he was after, and he wasn't above giving his ministry away to get results.

STARTING A RELATIONSHIP

Clearly, mentoring is a vital relationship. But how do you, as a leader, go about identifying whom to mentor? The following are some keys to remember as you begin the process.

Questions

God likes to set up mentoring relationships. I constantly ask him, "Is this one You're arranging, Lord?" Sometimes I become aware of it gradually, in a discussion or over a period of time. Other times I sense it instantly. On Sundays, I stand in the hall to greet people on their way into the church. Every once in a while, God will point someone out to me even if it's his or her first time at our church.

A few years back I met a young man with whom I briefly chatted. The Lord told me then and there that he was a church planter whom I would mentor. I sent someone to find out who the guy was, because there was something special about him. I was told he had just graduated as a lieutenant from West Point, the most respected military academy in the United States. He was an incredibly smart guy who was just starting seminary. I thought, *Ah! We got one!* I began meeting with him and we developed a relationship. He is now planting a church in a nearby city.

Those Hungry to Learn

I won't mentor people who are apathetic. I look for those who are eager, who I won't have to motivate, who already want what our relationship can yield. How do you find those types of young people? Simply take note of the people around you. Often the people right before your eyes—those who are pestering you, making trouble and asking the sticky questions—are the ones to invest in. They are trying to say "Pay attention to me. I want something from you. I want a little more relationship with you."

Those Who Share Your Vision

I look for people who I feel are destined to be fully trained pastors. I try to breed that kind of leader in my church. Some are beginning to understand what is going on and are taking the first steps. Eventually we must reach the stage in the Church where the elders mentor the youth in every possible calling.

Those with Whom You Have an Affinity

You must love them all, but you only like some. To mentor somebody, you need to like him or her because you will be spending a lot of time together. You may ask yourself, *What about the others?* Just match them up with somebody who gets along with them. You must be selective because you can't mentor everybody.

Someone with Unrealized Potential

It is absolutely essential that you mentor someone you can believe in, and you must communicate that belief to him or her. It is one of the most powerful things you can do. Jesus took one look at Peter—a rough, impulsive fisherman who had a few weaknesses—and said, "You are Peter, and on this rock I will build my Church" (Matthew 16:18). Of course, at that point Peter left everything to follow Jesus. Do you think he responded well to Jesus' confidence in him?

Believing in those you mentor and expressing that belief to them has the power to change them thoroughly. Many people never reach their potential because they have never sensed from others that they have worth. They are afraid to become who they are meant to be because they're afraid of failure. But having someone sincerely believe in them is incredibly powerful. Give God glory, and watch them become all they can be by believing in what God can do through them.

Ambassadors for Christ

The early Christians survived amidst the persecution of a pluralistic society similar to today. All kinds of religions competed for control and longevity and yet, the early Christians prevailed in impacting the world.

Historians will tell you that they simply outlived everybody else, but the truth is that they outthought everybody else and used their minds better than the rest. They outperformed everyone and had a powerful impact on every aspect of society. I hope to mentor a generation of young people who can continue that impact.

I try to get everyone in my church to be mentors in different ways. I tell the businesspeople not only to mentor people spiritually, but also in business—teach them how to do their work well. If you are an academic, teach those you mentor how to be good academics. If you are in the field of science, teach them the profession to the best of your ability. We must mentor young people in all areas, picking up on the spiritual parts as they come up. If you mentor nonbelievers, sooner or later they will run into a spiritual crisis and look to you for answers. It's important that you are ready and waiting.

Wherever you are, you are an ambassador for Christ. The people you work with might be pagans who despise the name of Jesus, but you can still serve them. Do not print up business cards that say "Counseling Service," or paint "Office Chaplain" on your door; simply be there in times of trouble. Consider them your people, and take care of them in every respect. Every individual eventually undergoes a spiritual crisis—that point where they reach the end of their rope and ask the deep questions. If you're there at that critical moment, having established yourself as a friend, they will listen to what you have to say, and you can offer them God's hope. They will end up owning your beliefs through a relational process, not an intellectual one. You couldn't do that if you decided just to mentor Christians.

Getting Started

Sometimes it can be difficult to know where to get started because not many people have been fortunate enough to witness this model personally. However, the following guidelines should help you as you begin your mentoring relationships:

- Continue to work on yourself. Never stop growing and learning. If you have a problem with insecurity, work through it.

- Identify the people you want to mentor, and invest in them. Pay attention to them, get to know them, talk to them and hang out with them.

- Assess each person's position. Ask the person what he or she is doing now. Then ask what he or she would like to be doing in 5 or 10 years. I ask these questions early on, sometimes at our first meeting. What they don't know is that I've already begun my assessment. For a relationship of this magnitude, I see where they're at, where they're headed and then ask myself whether I can help them get there. This assessment will help guide your next step.

- Take them with you as much as possible. Don't do anything alone. If you need to counsel someone, travel somewhere or do a planning meeting, take someone you are mentoring with you. When Jesus sent out the 72 and the 12 in Luke 10, He sent them out 2 by 2 and told them to preach what He had been preaching. It was an easy assignment because they had been traveling with Jesus and most likely knew all His messages by heart. Anyone who does a lot of speaking often uses the same talks over and over. The Gospel writers simply repeated what Jesus taught. Jesus traveled from village to village preaching the gospel. In the end, you know the disciples were at the back saying, "Here comes the sowing story!" and, "Oh boy, here's the leaven one! Here it comes!"

Just as the disciples benefited from hearing the same stories over and over, the things you teach those you mentor will only stick if they are around you enough to hear them more than once.

- Make them use their wings. Put them in situations where they must fly. If they aren't scared, then you're not moving them out enough. I like those I mentor to have a little fear in their lives. I want them to be uncertain, because that's when growth takes place and God takes over.

- Don't keep all the successes and failures for yourself. At one point God really spoke to me and said, "Look, you're being too protective. You're protecting them from mistakes too much. Get out of the way and let Me deal with your guys. This is how you learned, and it's how they will learn." I just had to take a little step back and let them do it. Some will disappoint you, but that's inevitable. Jesus didn't have a 100 percent success rate with His disciples either.

- Be mindful of their learning curve. The growth pattern for leaders consists of plateaus and jumps. They reach a certain level, acquire confidence, their capacities increase, and suddenly, they're ready for a higher level of responsibility and ministry. When that jump point is imminent, they get restless and may even start to sound a little disgruntled. They know something isn't quite right although they may not be sure what it is. When you sense that they're at that point, say, "I think it's time for you to take on more responsibility." Don't worry if moving them into a new position creates a void you will need to fill. That will get taken care of in time, especially if you are constantly training up new leaders.

- Ask them questions that make them think. When they ask questions, instead of giving a simple answer, ask them what they think the answer is. I'm famous for answering questions with more questions! I want my leaders to work through their problems and to understand all the bits and pieces that go into an answer.

- Be a cheerleader. Tell them, "You did great! That was wonderful! You're on the right track. You're a success." These words build the foundation for growth. As I mentioned earlier, recognition is a form of payment for a job well done.

Q & A

Question: How do I stop people from becoming too dependent on me?

Steve Nicholson: Make them tackle the tough issues and rely on God without doing things for them. Challenging and pushing them can build confidence. It helps them realize that God can use them and that they can do it without relying on you. Your determination to see them fly from the nest will help keep them from becoming too dependent on you.

In the beginning they ask me a lot of questions. When they first go out to lead a new church, they call me pretty often—sometimes every week! After a little while they begin to think, *I know what he's going to say.* They learn my thinking. As they pick up the phone to call me, they think, *I know what he'll say, but I'll just check.* Sure enough I will answer as they imagined. Pretty soon they stop calling and simply grow up. They soon assume my responses as their own. They begin with, "Somebody said . . . ," which later becomes, "It's always been said . . . ," and finally, "I've always said . . ." It's all part of the process of them leaving the nest.

Q: Do you ever experience problems with favoritism and jealousy if you're being selective with whom you mentor?

SN: Yes. People can feel left out when you devote large amounts of time to a small group. Part of me wants to say, "Well, that's tough." However, there are some measures you can take that could help.

First, I don't usually publicly name those I mentor unless I'm teaching about mentoring. I don't make a big deal in church about the time I spend with them. To a certain extent, I try to hide it.

Second, I am completely available to all members of the church. Even in a church of 700, anybody can meet with me if they ask. It might be two months down the road, but I never deny them. On Sundays, I hardly ever speak to the leaders so that I can be available to whoever is walking into church without partiality. I'll talk with them and pray with them—whatever the need—until they are all inside. The same is true when they leave after the service.

But during the week, when the eyes of the church are elsewhere, I play favorites ruthlessly. Not capriciously—it is not a matter of whim but of intention. In this way, my work with one person trickles down through the years to many more. I invest in people who then invest in others.

Q: I'm not so sure I can effectively mentor. As a new youth leader, I don't know what I'm doing. I have an older group and a younger group. How do I know when to start mentoring?

SN: It sounds pretty good so far! Look at the older group. When they hang out, who always makes the decisions? Who calls all the shots? There are always one or two. Spend time with them, invest in them and challenge them to set examples for the younger group. Put the older ones to work with the young ones. Voila! You are mentoring.

Q: Should those I mentor form their own friendships?

SN: Certainly. Many of them will become life-long friends. I look forward to the day when those I mentor will speak at each other's churches and help each other out at conferences, just like I do with my peers. It is wonderful to witness.

Q: I am working with someone on emotional and self-esteem issues. I don't think I'm getting through; I feel like we're going around in circles. What can I do?

SN: You might just have to back off and give them more time. Emotional and self-esteem issues are difficult to break through quickly. They take time. The most you can do is to encourage them in their relationship with God.

Q: How can you mentor the girls in leadership without experienced women in the church?

SN: I don't mentor women. You need to help the older women gain experience mentoring younger women. How? By throwing them in the ring—they must just start doing it. Turn them loose and they'll be fine. Women generally have less trouble with mentoring than men do. The female leaders are there, but make sure you allow them to realize their potential. You don't need to change your theology if that's an issue for you. Simply let them lead other women.

A REVOLUTIONARY APPROACH TO YOUTH MINISTRY!

The **Soul Survivor Encounter Kit** includes five *Real Life & Undignified Worship Student Magazines,* one *Real Life & Undignified Worship Leader's Guide,* one *Real Life & Undignified Worship DVD,* one *Soul Survivor Guide to Youth Ministry,* one *Soul Survivor Prayer Ministry* and one *Soul Survivor Guide to Service Projects.* ISBN 08307.35267

Soul Survivor is a dynamic British youth ministry that has impacted hundreds of thousands of young people worldwide through its powerful youth events for over 10 years. Soul Survivor has released such leaders as **Matt and Beth Redman** and **Tim Hughes**. With **Soul Survivor Encounter**, youth leaders around the world can use the successful elements of the Soul Survivor ministry to create in their young people a passionate commitment to worshiping God and to putting their faith into action.

The kit's relevant resources include contemporary student magazines with 12 interactive sessions, as well as leadership materials and intense DVD segments. Sessions feature interviews with leaders, artists and young people; quotations from pop culture; activities; devotional verses and Scripture discussions.

Soul Survivor Encounter gives youth leaders a radically **new** and **proven** way to reach young people for Christ. This biblical and relevant program is sure to ignite a revolution in youth ministry that will impact generations to come. Be a part of it!

Available at your local Christian bookstore
www.SoulSurvivorEncounter.com

 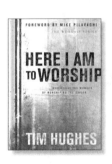  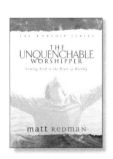  

ENERGIZE YOUR YOUTH GROUP WITH SOUL SURVIVOR ENCOUNTER

The cutting-edge Soul Survivor Encounter student magazines feature interviews with leaders, artists and young people; quotations from pop culture; activities; devotional verses and Scripture discussions. Each leader's guide provides leaders with everything they need to teach the interactive multimedia sessions in the student magazines. The DVDs contain clips to be used in conjunction with the magazines to reinforce each session topic.

Real Life & Undignified Worship Student Magazine

Includes six sessions that explore faith, evangelism, sin, the nature of God, why we need Him, and perseverance in the Christian life. It also includes six sessions on the biblical foundations of worship, the lifestyle of worship, intimacy, surrender and creativity in worship.

ISBN 08307.35364

Real Life & Undignified Worship Leader's Guide
ISBN 08307.35313

Real Life & Undignified Worship DVD
UPC 607135.008927

Soul in the City & Temptation Student Magazine

Features six sessions that explore justice—what the Bible says about justice; the poor and marginalized; prejudices; the Church under fire; models of justice; and justice in your community. The magazine also includes six sessions on purity and overcoming addictions—honest conversation about purity; purity every day; defining holiness; honesty, authenticity and accountability; the roots of addiction; forbidden fruit; and freedom from addiction.

ISBN 08307.35380

Soul in the City & Temptation Leader's Guide
ISBN 08307.35348

Soul in the City & Temptation DVD
UPC 607135.008941

Living the Life & Survivors Student Magazine

Explores evangelism as a lifestyle and includes sessions on the importance of relationships, storytelling, action and the Holy Spirit in turning our whole lives into acts of evangelism. The magazine also includes six sessions on a diverse group of biblical examples and renowned leaders including Job, Martin Luther, Paul, Mother Teresa, Joshua, Jonah, Corrie ten Boom, Ruth, Harriet Tubman and more. The stories of their lives serve as examples of obedience, worship, prayer, forgiveness, faith and compassion.

ISBN 08307.36565

Living the Life & Survivors Leader's Guide
ISBN 08307.36557

Living the Life & Survivors DVD
UPC 607135.009375